Melissa Ohden and the hundreds of other abortion survivors strike fear into the heart of the abortion industry because they are living proof of the lies the industry seeks to cover up. I should know, because I worked at Planned Parenthood for eight years. If nothing else, pick up this book if you're seeking the truth about abortion, about what happens to those who survive, and about the mercy and love of God so prevalent on every page. Whether pro-life or pro-choice, you'll know exactly what you support after reading *Abortion Survivors Break Their Silence*.

ABBY JOHNSON, author of *Unplanned* and Planned Parenthood director turned pro-life advocate

In a post–*Roe v. Wade* world, we are having conversations about the reality of abortion that we've never had before. One of those conversations is about those who have experienced something most of us could never imagine—surviving a brutal attempt to end their life through abortion. Melissa Ohden and Cindy Lambert shine a light on this little-talked-about aspect of the fight to defend the dignity of all human beings, and they beautifully give voice to these courageous individuals. As a physician, [I found] the stories of how abortion survivors impacted the lives of the medical professionals who cared for them [to be] especially impactful. *Abortion Survivors Break Their Silence* is a must-read for anyone who wants to understand more about the true toll abortion has had on our society and how we can care for the most vulnerable.

DR. CHRISTINA FRANCIS, CEO of the American Association of Pro-Life Obstetricians and Gynecologists

T0004917

Abortion Survivors Break Their Silence is a book that shines a light in the darkness. The stories of Melissa Ohden and the other survivors featured in this book are a testament to the power of resilience, faith, and love in the face of great adversity. If you want to be inspired to stand up for what is right and make a difference in the world, then read this book today.

DAVID BEREIT, author, speaker, and founder of 40 Days for Life

When society denies the basic existence of a group of people, we deny that those individuals are human beings made in the image of God. *Abortion Survivors Break Their Silence* challenges us to think more deeply about the serious impact and devastating effects of abortion. We are all made in the image of God, and each of us deserves to be treated with dignity and respect.

ROBYN CHAMBERS, Vice President of Advocacy for Children at Focus on the Family

ABORTION SURVIVORS BREAK THEIR SILENCE

ABORTION SURVIVORS BREAK THEIR SILENCE

MELISSA OHDEN

with Cindy Lambert

FOCUS
ON
THE FAMILY.

A Focus on the Family resource
published by Tyndale House Publishers

CONTENTS

TO MY COMMUNITY OF ABORTION SURVIVORS AROUND THE WORLD:

May this book show you that you are seen,
you are heard, and you are not alone.
Whether you break your silence publicly
or whisper it quietly, you matter.

FOREWORD

Abby Johnson

I KNOW WHAT IT'S LIKE TO FEEL UNSEEN, unheard, and lonely—like no one can possibly relate to what you've been through, what you've done, or what you've seen. I've experienced those intense feelings, and my friend Melissa Ohden did too when she found out she was the survivor of an attempted abortion. *Were there others like her? Where were they? What were their stories? Did they, too, feel unseen?*

When I quit my job at Planned Parenthood after seeing an ultrasound-guided abortion of a thirteen-week-old baby, I had similar questions: *Were there other abortion workers who left the industry? Had they seen what I'd seen, felt what I'd felt, done the same unspeakable things I had done?*

At first glance, it might seem like my story and Melissa's story are nothing alike. After all, I worked in an abortion clinic that ended the lives of babies, while Melissa survived the very procedure that my livelihood depended on. Yet our stories are not that different. In ways both expected and not, Melissa and I are very much alike. The biggest parallel? The mercy of God is at the center of both our stories.

By the time I left Planned Parenthood in 2009, Melissa Ohden had been telling her story for just a couple of years. She decided to speak up about her story not long after she found out she was an abortion survivor. I, meanwhile, was thrust into the spotlight only because Planned Parenthood filed a very public lawsuit against me after I left. (They lost, by the way.) I didn't have much time to heal from my work at Planned Parenthood, not to mention my own abortions, before I, too, started telling my story. Both of us experienced our own healing journeys while in the public eye. This was a shared history that bound us together before we ever met.

We started our nonprofit organizations the very same year, looking to offer ministry to those like us—those who felt they had no voice; those who felt utterly alone in their experiences.

Clinic workers are often overlooked in the abortion debate. They do their jobs behind closed doors—dispensing life-ending medications, holding the hands of distraught women, seeing things they cannot unsee. They are in desperate need of healing and a community of women who know exactly what they've been through.

The same is true of abortion survivors. They are also largely missing in the national debate. They are also in need of healing and fellowship with other survivors. For years they lacked a voice, but now, thanks to Melissa's ministry—The Abortion Survivors Network—they have one.

Everyone wants to be heard, right? Everyone wants to be seen, or at least not ignored. Everyone wants to be part of a community that understands them, that shares a common experience. The former abortion workers who engage with my ministry, And Then There Were None, are all part of a tribe. You will read about one such tribe member in chapter 3. Her name is Priscilla Hurley, and she is also an abortion survivor.

The fact is that we exist. Former abortion workers exist. Abortion survivors exist. The underbelly of the abortion industry is cruel, messy, and incredibly damaging to women and families. This industry would love nothing more than to suppress our voices, to silence all of us who tell the truth about what happens behind closed doors and about the heroic few who have saved babies like Melissa from certain death.

I can't tell you how much I appreciate Melissa's decision to bring the stories in this book to light. Though my story and the stories of survivors like Melissa are wildly different, we both want to expose what has been hidden for so long. We want the stories you'll read here to stick with you long after you've turned the last page. We want you to share this book with anyone and everyone you know. We want it to be a vehicle for the truth and for the unfathomable mercy of God.

When I think about Melissa, Priscilla, and all the other abortion survivors I know, I feel an immeasurable depth of gratitude to God for their lives. It was by the mercy of God that I left Planned Parenthood and can write this today. It was that same mercy and love that helped bring Melissa and me together in the campaign against abortion. May you recognize the same wondrous love of God throughout these pages and in your own life. And may you be encouraged to join us in the fight.

ABBY JOHNSON
PSALM 30

1

WHISPERED SECRETS

Attendees at the first Abortion Survivors Network retreat

"I'M ONE OF YOU."

Startled, having thought I'd found a rare moment of solitude on Canada's Parliament Hill, I spun around to find the source of the whispering voice behind me. There, in the previously bustling location of the 2010 March for Life, stood a young man. Nothing about him stood out. He appeared safe, so I wasn't alarmed.

His words, however, puzzled me. Did he know who I was? Had he been there earlier that day when I told my story to the huge crowd that gathered before the march began? And what did he mean by "I'm one of you"? Perhaps he'd seen my knees buckle in grief as I marched past one of the abortion clinics operated by the infamous Canadian abortionist Dr. Henry Morgentaler. Did he just want me to know that he, too, was passionate about protecting the lives of the unborn?

"Do I know you?" I replied cautiously. *This is going to go one of two ways,* I thought. *He's going to be embarrassed by having whispered that to me, possibly mistaking me for someone else. Or, if he meant what I suspect, our worlds are about to be rocked by this meeting.*

He smiled. "I know who you are. You're an abortion survivor. I'm one too."

Not only was he *not* mistaken about my identity—we shared the same identity!

I moved closer and saw that his eyes reflected my own sense of wonder. This was the first time in my life I'd ever come face-to-face with another abortion survivor. My heart rate quickened as anticipation swept over me. Was I really about to trade survival stories with someone who, like me, had survived an effort to snuff out his life before he'd taken his first breath?

I studied his face as if trying to discern his story through his appearance. He looked young—younger than my thirty-three years.

Sensing the curiosity in my eyes, he began to tell me his story. He was twenty-one. An adoptee, like me, he had learned the truth about his birth story only one year earlier, when he'd met his biological mother. He turned around to show me the back of his head, which was visibly flattened from what he was told was an injury sustained during the attempted abortion.

I was surprised by his story, and maybe even more so by his bravery in sharing it. After all, wasn't I a stranger? Yet we both understood that we had so much in common. We were both members of a select group—a band of often silent, often overlooked, often disbelieved individuals whose stories don't fit the predominant narrative that abortion is all about the mother and her freedom of choice.

We didn't have much time that May afternoon (we both had to rush off to other events associated with the march), so we took turns sharing our survival stories, our words tumbling out excitedly and our heads nodding in understanding. Our short time together had a profound impact on me. I felt validated. Seen. Understood. I suspect it did the same for him, for there is great power in recognizing that you are not alone.

Alone. I've been there.

OUR FAMILY SECRET

I can still recall the bitter memories from the first time in my life I felt truly alone. I was fourteen years old and had just started eighth grade. My older sister, Tammy, was a high school junior, and we'd both grown up knowing we were adopted. Our parents were thoughtful and wise in how they explained it to us at an early age: We always knew they had chosen us to be their very own children, and we'd both been taught that our birth mothers loved us very much. That's why, since our birth mothers were unable to care for us, they entrusted us to Mom and Dad to be loved and raised in a wonderful family.

But my eighth-grade year added new complexities to our family dynamic. It was the fall of 1991, and my parents discovered that Tammy was pregnant. To their credit, Mom and Dad showed no anger at this development. It was clear that they were disappointed—they didn't try to hide it—but they demonstrated love and support for Tammy, along with a commitment to help her figure out what came next. Would she give her child up for adoption, as her birth mother had done? Would she keep and raise the child—and, if so, how would she do so? Or would she follow the path of so many other teenage moms and end the life of her baby?

My parents made it clear that they were on the side of life. They wanted Tammy to understand that every life is precious, that every child (born or unborn) has value and purpose. Unbeknownst to me, in their efforts to help Tammy see that every life matters—no matter how inconvenient—they revealed to Tammy a long-held secret about *me*. It was a secret that even I did not know. I don't know exactly how they told her, but Tammy was apparently so moved by it that she decided to keep and raise her baby with the help of our family.

I had no idea that my own hidden past had played a part in her decision until, shortly thereafter, during a heated argument between us, Tammy blurted out in anger: "At least my parents wanted me!"

I describe that moment in my book *You Carried Me: A Daughter's Memoir*.

"What's that supposed to mean?" I replied. Both of our birth mothers had wanted us—that's how we came to be adopted! I couldn't figure out what she was talking about. It was just Tammy spouting off.

But as I turned to face her, I saw that it was much more than that. The look of compassion and sisterly affection on her face at that moment was something I hadn't seen in a long time.

"You don't know? You really don't know, do you?" she said.

I stared at her in confusion. "Know what? What are you talking about?"

Tammy's face crumpled; it looked like a balloon after it pops. Quietly she said, "Wait for Mom and Dad to come home. Ask them, and you will see."

And so I waited.

Mom was the first one home. It was already dark when I met her at the door. The words spilled out of me as I told her about my fight with Tammy, and what she had said. My biggest worry was that I would be scolded for arguing with my sister; I was completely unprepared for what came next.

Mom and I made our way into the dimly lit living room. We sat knee-to-knee, Mom on the sofa, me on the adjacent love seat.

Mom's voice was soft and low as she took my hands in hers. "We never meant to keep this from you. . . . We should have told you when we told Tammy, but there was just no easy way. . . . We love you, honey, we'll always love you. . . ." She paused and took a deep breath. "Missy, your birth mother had an abortion during her pregnancy with you and you survived."

I sat for a moment in utter disbelief—how was this even possible? And then I fell into my mom's arms and sobbed.[1]

That's when the loneliness kicked in.

I hounded my parents with questions in the days that followed, but they had little additional information. They knew I had entered the world at St. Luke's Regional Medical Center in Sioux City, Iowa; that after my delivery I was set aside and left for dead; and that a nurse heard me whimper and saved my life. Naturally I wanted to know more, but that was all they knew.

This closely held secret, once revealed, defined my life from that point forward. At first I was angry, feeling betrayed and misled. I thank God, however, that those angry feelings eventually gave way to an even deeper closeness between my mother and me—a closeness that remains to this day. I marvel at how tenderly and wisely my parents handled my identity crisis after this shocking revelation.

My parents were a huge support to me as I continued my search for answers about my history in the years that followed. And they weren't the only ones I drew closer to—I found solace in my faith in God, which became more essential and more personal than ever. Yet in spite of this enhanced closeness with God and my parents, a sense of aloneness as an abortion survivor took root in my soul.

But now comes the good news! God used those feelings of isolation as a driving force in my life. Those feelings drove me to learn more about my origin story and to connect with my birth family. Those feelings drove me to become a voice in our culture who raises awareness of abortion survivors so that others can see that every life matters. Those same feelings also drove me to connect with other survivors and help them break their silence—so that they, too, can bear witness to the value of every life.

Until that afternoon in May 2010, when I met a young stranger on Canada's Parliament Hill, I'd never laid eyes on another survivor. Imagine the connection I felt when I learned his story. It didn't matter that I didn't know his name or where he was from. I knew his *identity* as a survivor—an identity he was eager to share with me. Relief washed over me as I learned that I was not alone in the circumstances of my birth—circumstances that cause some to call us a "dreaded complication."

"THE DREADED COMPLICATION"

I first came across that unflattering language in a news clipping dating back to 1981. In August of that year, the *Philadelphia Inquirer* published a watershed article on the largely unreported issue of abortions that result in live births. The article got its headline from the words of leading abortion expert and maternal-fetal specialist Dr. Thomas Kerenyi, who referred to an aborted fetus surviving outside the womb as "the dreaded complication."[2]

As dehumanizing as that term is, how can one blame an abortionist for viewing survivors this way? An abortionist's job is to end the life of a child in the womb. When an abortion fails, either by an error on the part of the doctor or through an unexplainable act of divine intervention, a surviving child certainly is a complication for those responsible. According to the *Inquirer* article's subtitle, "when a crying baby emerges and not a lifeless fetus, doctors have a problem with no easy answer."[3]

No easy answer, indeed.

In discussing saline-infusion abortions, which were performed routinely in the 1970s and 1980s and resulted in a number of live births, Dr. Kerenyi stated that "it's almost a breach of contract" to not administer a lethal dose of saline solution. "Otherwise, what are you going to do—hand her back a baby having done it questionable damage?"[4]

I eventually discovered that survival stories like mine have occurred throughout history, even prior to the legalization of abortion in many places, and have been whispered about in the dark corners of the abortion industry.

I've learned that the existence of abortion survivors was discussed more openly decades ago. Yet after some fifty years of legalized abortion—as characterizations of abortion as a protected right have shaped our culture, and as abortion has increasingly polarized American society—the existence of survivors is barely mentioned. The truth has been swept so far under the rug that abortion survivors are silenced, shamed, or just plain ignored. The same is true about almost anyone whose experience doesn't support the popular narrative that abortion is synonymous with women's empowerment.

Despite statements by family members and medical professionals, evidence in the form of medical and adoption records, and the existence of so many survivors, the predominant message is that failed abortions don't happen and that these survivors don't exist. Even when confronted with our names, our faces, and our stories, many in the media and in politics continue to insist that we're fairy tales—a figment of imagination concocted to overturn legalized abortion. This messaging comes down from the top—from pro-choice activists and leaders in the abortion industry—and it dominates the conversation.

For instance, writing for the online publication *Quartz*, reporter Annalisa Merelli stated that "an abortion is performed with the intention of ending a pregnancy, so there are no survivors."[5] When debating legislation that would require medical care for babies born alive after failed abortions, Irish politician Kate O'Connell referred to abortion survivors as "alleged survivors of botched abortions" and suggested that such stories are made up. She said those advocating for born-alive infants were "listening to anecdotes, fairy tales, and, I mean essentially, stories that, you know, have dubious sources."[6] Calla Hales, an activist and abortion clinic director for multiple facilities, made this claim in 2019: "There are major issues with 'born alive' bills. First, they're entirely based on propaganda. It is highly unlikely for an abortion to result in a live birth."[7]

This is how many of our stories have been viewed. First, our existence as abortion survivors was often kept secret from us, even by our families. (Having now worked with more than five hundred survivors, I can attest to how common this is.) Second, our existence was also kept secret by the abortionists and nurses who were firsthand witnesses to our failed abortions. We have now progressed—or, more appropriately, *regressed*—to where the abortion industry and politicians view our existence as a potential threat to abortion on demand.

I find it surreal that I actually survived an abortion, and this revelation was an emotionally, mentally, and physically traumatic experience. But then to be marginalized, doubted, discounted, silenced, and downright ignored? It's like being traumatized all over again. Survivors like me bear witness to the devastation of abortion, yet the world around us seems determined to deny our plight.

In the midst of the silence, however, there are whispers. Whispers of truth. Whispers of experience. Whispers like the one shared with me on Parliament Hill: "I'm one of you."

THE POWER OF STORIES

It is time to stop the whispering. It is time to speak up and speak out. It is time to tell our stories aloud for all to hear. Why? Because abortion—and the existence and experiences of abortion survivors—affects so many of us: from the mothers and fathers who arranged an abortion only to have their child survive; to extended family members and adoptive families who have raised a survivor or simply kept the secret; to medical professionals, clinic staff, adoption workers, and more.

This book is about survivors breaking their silence by telling their stories. Why are they breaking their silence *now*? Perhaps the better question is *Who else will tell their stories?* Moreover, who will *listen* to what were once just whispers spoken in the darkness of fear and shame?

Survivors are breaking their silence because doing so empowers them. Survivors are breaking their silence because the world desperately needs to hear their stories. Survivors are breaking their silence, as hard as it often is, because they have hope—hope that others affected by abortion might break their silence as well. Hope that maybe, as we break our silence, fewer people will fall prey to the false messages that abortion is a human right, that abortions don't fail, and that survivors don't exist.

Stories have power. A story does more than challenge the intellect—it moves the heart. It opens eyes. It takes up residence in the mind of the hearer. It works on the spirit. God filled His Word with stories. Jesus captivated crowds with stories because He knew that stories often stay with us even after sermons are forgotten. Stories are memorable and shareable.

Though I never again saw that young man I encountered in Canada, the story of our meeting stayed with me. It helped shape my ministry. It taught me the impact of survivors sharing their stories with one another. I'll never forget the moment when he turned to the side and showed me the flattened back of his head—the evidence of his injury in the womb at the hand of an abortionist. That same story is now a part of your memory—it's a story that you, too, can share.

I'm sure you've noticed, as I have, that when we hear a story, we are prone to look for villains, victims, and heroes. And oh, how we love to hate the villains! I confess that I once viewed my own story in these terms, and you may be tempted to do the same as you read this book. It's easy to do.

But I urge you to resist that temptation. Whenever you think you spot a villain in our stories, I implore you to look more closely and see what Jesus sees—a flawed human heart in need of mercy and love. Look beyond the apparent deception and selfishness and disregard for life (you will likely spot all three in my story), and see instead the woman brought before Jesus—a woman who had been caught in adultery. How did Jesus treat her when the scribes and Pharisees were ready to throw their stones? He challenged the woman's would-be executioners with the words "Let him who is without sin among you be the first to throw a stone at her" (John 8:7). And one by one, her accusers walked away.

I'll admit that as I heard some of the stories you are about to read and pieced together the details of my own story, I had a stone in my hand. And why not? After all, I view myself as a champion of the unborn and the just-born. Are those who promote and participate in abortion not villains to be condemned? Isn't it only fair to condemn those who plotted my death or participated in the attempt on my life? If they'd had their way, I'd be dead. What's more, millions of babies are dead because those like the villains in my story did have their way. It's only natural to condemn them, right?

Yes, it is natural. But Jesus doesn't call us to act naturally. He calls us to follow Him, and that means to follow His example. He taught us to forgive, to demonstrate grace, and to extend unconditional love.

I did not write this book to add fuel to the fire that rages over abortion. That fire devours and destroys. It heightens tempers, shuts down dialogue, obscures understanding, and obliterates love. No, it is not my desire to further polarize our divided culture.

Instead, I wrote this book to highlight the grace of our wondrous God in the midst of our very broken, dark world. I have written it to show that every person's story is, in fact, a love story. Returning to John 8, what does Jesus say in verse 12, right after demonstrating unconditional love and grace to the woman caught in adultery? "I am the light of the world. Whoever follows me will not walk in darkness, but will have the light of life."

So as you read the stories that follow, take note of each time you find yourself picking up a figurative stone to throw. Drop it. Instead, look for the grace on display in that story. Then find a way to help break the silence. Tell a friend about what God did to save a life, to mend broken relationships, to heal bitter hearts, and to conquer hatred with love.

2

MORE THAN A CHOICE: MY STORY

Melissa Ohden with her birth mother, Ruth

"HOW COULD YOU BE SO CARELESS? How could you let this happen?" Helen screamed at her daughter, Ruth, and her daughter's fiancé, Elliott, as they cowered before her. Ruth, a nineteen-year-old college student, had just learned that she was carrying me.

Ruth and Elliott had dated through high school and into college, and now their newly hatched plan—upon learning of my existence—was to marry before I was born and raise me together. Helen, however, would entertain no thoughts of such a marriage. "I'll take care of this!" she shouted—clearly meaning the pregnancy, not a wedding. The matter was not open to debate. The young couple's hopes to marry and raise me were dashed to pieces during the confrontation with Helen. Moreover, that same confrontation was the last time Ruth and Elliott would ever see one another.

When we hear the story of a young, pregnant woman, we often learn of her fear and trepidation over telling her parents about her pregnancy. Yet Ruth never experienced that inner turmoil because it was her mother who first realized Ruth was pregnant. Ruth never even suspected. She was training with her college volleyball team when she conceived, so when her menstrual cycle became erratic and then stopped, she assumed it was due to intense exercise. So when her twin sister, also her college roommate, expressed concern that Ruth was frequently hot and kept opening their dorm room window, Ruth simply dismissed it, unaware that I was already growing inside her.

In August 1977, Ruth was visiting her home in South Sioux City, Nebraska, preparing to return to college at the University of South Dakota. Her mother, Helen, was an ob-gyn nurse, nurse educator, and supervisor. Helen recognized the signs and symptoms of pregnancy that Ruth didn't. Thus Ruth learned of her own pregnancy from her mother, who angrily confronted her.

As the news made its way through the extended family, several members offered to let Ruth reside with them during her pregnancy, but her furious mother rebuffed all offers.

Mere days after the heartrending confrontation, Ruth arrived at St. Luke's Regional Medical Center, bypassing normal hospital regulations and procedures. Her mother, who supervised many of the nursing students, wielded considerable influence there. I've since learned, from the accounts of those close to Helen and some of the nursing students, that the local abortionist, who also delivered babies as an ob-gyn, owed Helen a "really big favor." That's apparently how my abortion was arranged outside standard policy and against my birth mother's will. My medical records state that Ruth was an estimated "18–20 weeks pregnant." At that stage of pregnancy, Ruth should have been required to go before a hospital committee to present her case for the procedure, even if her reasoning was based on mental health.

But there was no committee appearance. There was no discussion of Ruth's wants or needs. There was no consideration of Elliott's wishes. And there was certainly no consideration of what was best for the person growing inside Ruth: me.

On August 24, 1977, a hospital worker started a saline infusion for my abortion. Typically this procedure takes a matter of hours. Typically—but not in Ruth's case. Over the next five days, Ruth suffered intense physical and emotional pain as the saline infusion surged through her womb. There's little doubt that I suffered excruciating pain as the saline worked to poison me—to essentially scald me to death.

Saline infusions were probably the most common abortion procedure in the 1970s. Although they resulted in tens of millions of children being aborted, they also resulted in a significant number of live births, which ultimately led to abortion survivors being branded the "dreaded complication" as discussed in chapter 1.

(Sadly, the number of abortion survivors like me and the hundreds of others I've connected with led the abortion industry to search for much more effective—in other words, more lethal—methods to ensure that children like me aren't accidentally born alive. This led to the eventual development of procedures such as partial-birth abortion.)

Hospital staffers made numerous attempts over those five long days to induce Ruth's labor, to ultimately expel me from the womb as a successfully aborted, deceased child. I'll never know whether it was some subconscious stubbornness on my part to not budge from the womb (as I sometimes wonder), but the reality is that I was left to soak in that toxic solution for *days* rather than the typical few hours. With each passing day, the concern over Ruth's well-being grew.

I later learned that her twin sister was alerted that Ruth's life could be in danger, so she attempted to sneak Ruth out of the hospital in an effort to save her. Caught in the act, Ruth's twin was warned that it was too late. Any attempt to stop the abortion would put Ruth's health at further risk, she was told. Furthermore, there was no hope in trying to save the baby. No turning back now.

I can only imagine the anguish of the hospital staff who witnessed Ruth's ordeal over those five days. I suspect they knew that this was *not* Ruth's choice. I often wonder if Helen or the abortionist felt any anguish as the procedure lingered on, days longer than expected or intended. Did they worry for Ruth's survival? Did they feel guilty as they watched her suffer? Did either of them worry about losing their jobs—or their licenses—if their actions were discovered? There must have been moments of fear during those gruesome five days.

Finally, on August 29, Ruth's labor was successfully induced. The doctor and Helen were surely relieved that labor was in progress, but, of course, they expected to see a dead baby. Can you imagine their shock when I emerged from the birth canal alive? They were suddenly faced with horrific choices. Would they treat me as a tiny patient in need of immediate medical intervention, or would they set me aside to die? Would they be honest with my birth mother about my condition, or would they lead her to believe that the abortion was successful?

I've since learned that they told Ruth not to look as I was delivered; that I was a hideous monster. They even told her the abortion was successful—that I was dead. Ruth was afraid to ask if I was a girl or a boy, and neither her mother nor the doctor volunteered the information. Unbeknownst to Ruth, they simply set me aside to die.

Many years later I found and spoke with a nurse who was

present at my delivery. (She remembered the nurse who saved me but did not recall her name.) Not only did Helen make it clear to the nurses that I was to be left unattended, but no one was to ever tell my birth mother the truth or they would regret it. My heart still breaks for those nurses. They were placed in an agonizing position: unwilling accomplices to deception and a total disregard for the suffering of a tiny, dying baby.

I owe my life to a tall, blonde nurse. I still don't know her name, and will likely never know all that happened that day, but I do know that she rushed me to the hospital's neonatal intensive care unit (NICU). According to my medical records, my newborn Apgar (appearance, pulse, grimace, activity, and respiration) score shows that I was near death five minutes after delivery. I weighed two pounds, fourteen ounces, which indicated to the medical professionals that my birth mother was much further along in her pregnancy than the eighteen to twenty weeks the abortionist had suggested. In fact, a neonatologist remarked in my records that he estimated me to be about thirty-one weeks along. (In my years of research and working with survivors of failed abortions, I've discovered that many of the babies who survive abortion attempts do so because the abortionist was either wrong in estimating their gestational age or didn't perform an adequate exam to determine their gestational age.)

I remained in the NICU at St. Luke's for twenty-one days, and was then transferred to another hospital. I suffered from severe respiratory and liver problems as well as seizures. For a time the doctors thought I had a fatal heart defect because of the signs of distress I was showing. They were guarded about what my future might hold— their predictions included both physical and mental disabilities. There were so many unknowns. It is likely that Helen was unaware of any of this, since by this point I was considered abandoned.

Ruth returned to her mother's home, heartbroken over losing both me and Elliott. She never knew I was alive, much less that by God's grace, I was surrounded by attentive nurses who cared for me, prayed over me, and delighted in watching me survive and— eventually—thrive. Years later I learned that some of those nurses never forgot me.

When it became clear that I would survive, I was made a ward of the state. I was adopted by loving parents who nurtured and cared for me. My adoptive parents had no idea that the adoption was arranged without Ruth's knowledge or consent, and that the mother's signature on the paperwork was not the mother's hand-writing at all. Little did they know that my birth mother would spend the next thirty years grieving the death of a child she was forced to abort.

GOING PUBLIC

While Ruth was grieving, I grew up knowing I was both adopted and deeply loved. You've already read about how, as a teenager, I accidentally found out about the attempted abortion, like many survivors do. I was devastated when I learned the truth about my past. I didn't want to be a survivor. I felt ashamed and embar-rassed, guilty for surviving when millions of others haven't been so fortunate. I began to work through the anger and resentment I felt toward my birth parents—not knowing the full story—and although it was a process, I began to forgive them. I still continue on my journey of forgiveness today. (I recount the full journey in *You Carried Me*.)

In 1996, when I was nineteen (the same age as Ruth when she discovered she was pregnant with me), I set out to learn more about my past. During the next eleven years, I also listened to lots of people's stories—first as a teacher, then as a children's advocate, then as a therapist, then as a supervisor in social service settings—but none of those stories involved other abortion survivors. I felt terribly alone in my experience as an outlier. Eventually I stumbled across Gianna Jessen's story. Gianna is an abortion survivor who first went public with her story in the 1990s. Her experience eased my pain a little. Knowing there was at least one other survivor like me brought me solace.

Still, I knew no one with a story like mine to whom I could turn for support, no one outside my innermost circle who would hear me and understand. Then one group in particular took a chance on me: Feminists for Life. They acknowledged me and my story, providing me with a platform for my voice and the opportunity to serve as an advocate for survivors. They gave me strength and courage.

So in 2007, at the age of thirty, I began publicly sharing my story as an abortion survivor. I still had no inkling of the number of failed abortions or how many survivors there were around the world. It was only after others heard my story that they began telling me their own experiences. In hindsight, it makes absolute sense: The same fear, shame, and loneliness that I felt for so long was lessened when I found out about Gianna Jessen. In the same way, hearing *my* story gave other survivors the strength and courage to tell me theirs. In a world that has, by and large, turned a blind eye to abortion survivors, we desperately need each other. Whom else can we turn to? Who else will understand us? That's why, when I began telling my story, others like me also found their voices. And we eventually found each other.

That same year, after much digging, I discovered the identity of my birth parents and obtained my medical records. At thirty years old, I finally read these disturbing words: "A saline infusion for an abortion was done but was unsuccessful." Once I learned who my birth father was, I discovered that both of us lived in South Sioux City, Nebraska—just across the Missouri River from Sioux City, Iowa, where my failed abortion took place. Even so, I wasn't yet ready to seek him out.

I was, however, ready to begin sharing (with permission, of course) the stories of other survivors who'd contacted me and providing information about failed abortions to pro-life leaders and anyone in the media who would listen.

HOW MANY?

When it comes to estimating the number of abortion survivors, we have to begin with the premise that few involved in the abortion practice are eager to report the truth. According to "Abortion: The Dreaded Complication," the 1981 *Philadelphia Inquirer* special report cited in chapter 1, "[Abortion live births] are little known because organized medicine, from fear of public clamor and legal action, treats them more as an embarrassment to be hushed up than a problem to be solved."[1]

In the words of Dr. Willard Cates, former head of abortion surveillance activities for the Centers for Disease Control and Prevention (CDC), reporting these live births is "like turning yourself in to the IRS for an audit. What is there to gain? The tendency is not to report because there are only negative incentives."[2]

Cates, however, did tell the *Inquirer* that as of the early 1980s, an estimated four to five hundred unintended live births occurred every year in the United States. According to the *Inquirer*, "That is only a tiny fraction of the nation's 1.5 million annual abortions. Still, it means that these unintended live births are literally an everyday occurrence."[3]

It's important to note that any currently available numbers almost certainly underestimate the *total* number of abortion survivors, because they invariably include data reported only from hospitals and do *not* include information from other abortion facilities.

Abortionist Kermit Gosnell, for example, was reportedly responsible for hundreds of "snippings" (referencing his practice of severing the spinal cords of living infants in order to kill them after delivering them alive), yet he did not report even one. His numbers alone exceed any definitive numbers provided by the CDC.[4]

And infants born alive after failed abortion attempts are not unique to the United States. As of 2021, my organization, The Abortion Survivors Network (ASN), has connected with abortion survivors from twenty different countries. There are a handful of countries that report the number of abortion survivors. For instance, the Canadian Institute for Health Information (CIHI) released reports reflecting that 766 babies were born alive during late-term abortions in Canada between 2013 and 2018.[5] In Australia, there were 27 reported survivors from 1999 to 2016.[6]

(Keep in mind that this is simply a glimpse of what we at ASN have learned. For example, available statistics don't take into account babies who survived at-home or illegal abortions. Nor do they include babies who survived abortions that took place before the practice was legalized in countries outside the United States.)

I remember giving an interview in Australia in 2010 and mentioning that hundreds, if not thousands, of abortion survivors exist around the world. The interviewer later wrote that it was "creepy" to hear this. I thought *creepy* was an odd word choice, especially considering that this journalist was friendly to the cause of life.

Like so many others, though, he found it alarming to learn the truth about survivors when the predominant narrative says we don't exist at all.

A NETWORK OF SURVIVORS

If there are indeed so many abortion survivors, where are they? Why haven't we heard more of their stories? I can assure you that we're out there. We absolutely do exist. More often than not, however, our secrets are known to very few. How many survivors are unaware of their own histories? And of those who do know the truth, many feel alone and ashamed—scared to tell their stories, whether from pressure or a lack of support from their own families or because they've read the claims that they and other purported survivors are lying. Mostly they're just trying to heal—to find someone who will listen, someone who will believe them, someone who will value them. After all, we live in a culture that is vehemently pro-choice—a culture that places a higher value on a woman's "right to choose" than on the right to be born and to live.

My mere existence, plus that of my fellow survivors, is a flaw in the arguments of so-called pro-choicers. Our births, our fights for survival, our collective voice, are a huge shout-out to the world: "We are more than the choice of others! We are humans in our own right, and we choose to live!"

Even as an injured newborn, whether I realized it or not, I chose to live. I arrived in this world fighting to breathe, fighting to survive. It was instinctive. This book describes others like me whose instincts to hold on to life, even by a thread, only add to that unified chorus: "I choose to live!"

Some survivors still don't know the truth, as their families have kept their survival stories a secret. Others know about their survival but don't have a lot of details. Based on my extensive experience, I've found that many survivors have no idea there are others like them.

In 2012, after years of hearing these whispered stories, I founded ASN to help provide social and emotional support to abortion survivors and their families. We created a first-of-its-kind healing curriculum, and we're on the front lines in offering a supportive environment for all who've been devastated by abortion. We also provide education and training in areas like public speaking.

In 2013 I moved to Kansas City, Missouri. I later learned that my birth mother and one of my half sisters lived there as well! Some members of my birth mother's family knew I had survived my abortion, and they had kept it a secret all those years. It wasn't until I started sharing my story publicly that they finally told Ruth the truth. By this point I was thirty-six years old.

How I wish I could have been a fly on the wall for that revelation! Still, I've heard Ruth describe what it was like: "Finding out that my baby had survived was just blinding—pure shock at first. I went numb. My twin sister, who broke the news to me, was still talking, but I couldn't hear her words. It was like the vault with my deepest secret was unlocked, and light started to pour in. I was overwhelmed with joy that the baby had survived, that she was healthy and thriving with a family of her own. I immediately wondered if it would be possible to find her, to meet her and get to know her, but I was also terrified that she would want nothing to do with me. I didn't know what, if anything, she knew about me and the terrible things that had happened to us."

I'm grateful to say that Ruth didn't have to wait too long for answers. Our face-to-face meeting was a moment of redemption and reconciliation! I got chills when she said to me, "Melissa, for years I struggled with deep regrets and shame. Why hadn't I run away to save my baby? Why hadn't I fought harder against my mother? I learned to live with the horrible emotional pain that my compliance had caused your death—a pain that never healed."

Her words washed over me. They flowed into my old wounds, bringing healing, peace, and restoration. When I first learned that I had survived an abortion, I never fathomed that my birth mother had truly loved me and longed for me. Now that I knew, my heart was stirred with a new empathy. Just as Ruth spent almost her entire pregnancy unaware of my existence, she likewise spent most of her life not knowing I had survived the procedure. It felt like my heart grew larger as we talked.

Ruth is now healing from her past and is a huge part of my life. After being united with my birth mother, my two half sisters, Jenny and Sarah, and a cousin (who connected us all and thus broke our family's silence), I learned that it wasn't the abortionist who demanded I be left to die that day—it was Ruth's mother, Helen. And with that knowledge, I needed to embark on a new journey of forgiveness. God helped me see that I'd picked up a stone to throw. He asked me to drop that stone, and to instead see Helen as an individual loved by Jesus.

As I was writing this book, I asked Ruth to describe her thoughts and feelings after our reunion. She told me, "Over time I cycled through all the stages—anger at what had happened to us, grief that I wasn't able to be there for you as you grew up."

She explained what she'd gone through over the years: "My mother told me to never speak of this terrible shame I had brought on the family. So I didn't. I never told my husband, who I married a year after you were taken from me. I never told my other daughters as they grew up. I never discussed it with friends, and certainly not with my family. I locked all that pain and trauma inside my heart, and I carried that enormous weight all alone for decades. Even though I did my best to live my life, to start over, to be a good wife and mother, I always felt like a piece was missing from the complete picture of my life. Looking back now, I wonder how different my life, and my mental health, could have been if I'd had a way to deal with all those things in a positive way."

Her words capture well what so many women who were compelled to get abortions—by parents, boyfriends, financial and social pressures—have endured. (Tragically, this still happens today.) But Ruth's next words are a testimony to the power of love and healing!

"Melissa, as we started getting to know each other, my heart knew that I had found my missing piece. Getting to know you, my first daughter, and your beautiful family has truly been a transformative joy in my life."

Yes—a transformative joy! Those words capture my experience as well.

SHARING OUR STORIES

These days, my husband and I still live in Kansas City with our two daughters, Ava and Olivia. I'm grateful they know my birth mother as "Grandma Ruth" and are being raised alongside their cousins. Along the way, I've also been united with other members of my extended family, on both my birth mother's and my birth father's sides. (Sadly, my birth father, Elliott, passed away before I had an opportunity to meet him.)

My story may be filled with tragedy and heartbreak, but it's also filled with great beauty—the beauty of a life spared from death, of a heroic nurse who risked her career to rescue me, of praying hospital workers, of loving and supportive adoptive parents, of the truth breaking through after decades of deception, and of forgiveness and reconciliation triumphing over guilt, blame, and bitterness. It is, in truth, a love story.

Realizing that my story is a love story has inspired me to reach out to other survivors, to help them discover their own love stories through the encouragement of ASN. As of the writing of this book, ASN now has been contacted by more than 545 abortion survivors (or families and friends who have communicated on their behalf) from around the world. These survivors range in age from infants to those in their eighties, who survived at-home abortion attempts before the procedure was legal. Every one of these souls is precious, and we know they represent only the beginning of this ministry.

In 2021, ASN held our first annual face-to-face retreat for abortion survivors, with seventeen in attendance, including myself. Also in 2021, ASN began equipping survivors who feel called to publicly share their stories of healing and empowerment.

It has been an exciting journey—from feeling completely alone as a survivor to finding a community of others who understand my past like no one else. In this community, we are able to share our unique stories and give one another strength, encouragement, and hope.

This book is an invitation to take a peek into this special community. You will see for yourself the value of each precious life that was spared. You'll discover with awe how God poured reconciliation and forgiveness into lives that you'd otherwise expect to find full of sadness, heartbreak, and bitterness. You'll understand why it is so important to tell these stories—because they remind us of the humanity of *every* human being. You'll learn why the term *abortion survivor* represents so much more than what's typically reported in the media. You'll see how survivor stories involve not just a mother and an unwanted baby, but all the lives that intersect theirs—the biological father, extended family members, nurses, doctors, and medical staff—particularly those who helped save a newborn often clinging to life—and, finally, the adoptive parents who grapple not only with potentially serious health issues but also with how and when to share the truth of their child's beginnings. Yes, each story of survival has many layers beneath the surface.

As you read, you'll also learn how these stories connect with yours. Because whether you're an abortion survivor or not, you, too, are so much more than someone else's choice. *Every* person is more than a choice. *Every* unborn child is more than a choice. Given the opportunity to live, it is in our very nature to express our own choice, in our own voice: "I want to live!"

Once again, a word of caution: If, while you're reading, you find yourself picking up a stone to throw—please, be sure to put it back down.

I hope you find within these pages both courage and inspiration, and may the words that follow shine a light on the darkness of abortion, exposing lies and illuminating this world with the true light of *life*.

And when you're done reading, let's walk together with survivors and their families as they seek support and healing. Bringing about cultural change takes time, so don't be discouraged. It happens one life, one story, at a time. It is my prayer that as you read and share the stories that follow, you will become a participant in changing our culture, helping those around you recognize that every human life is precious. Every life deserves respect and dignity. And every life is far more than a choice.

3

A LIFE REDEFINED: PRISCILLA'S STORY

Priscilla

THE WOUNDS AND DESTRUCTION OF ABORTION once defined Priscilla Hurley's life: first as a survivor of an incomplete abortion, next as a woman who twice experienced abortion, and finally as an abortion clinic worker.[1] In the beginning, she had no idea that her troubled inner life—filled with profound and complicated feelings of deep hurt, anger, grief, despair, confusion, and fear—was so closely tied to abortion.

Priscilla's life, even before birth, was filled with multiple traumas.

Her biological father (we'll call him Harold) was tall, dark, and wildly attractive, a charismatic and funny man with a happy smile. He was made, in aviation terms, of "the right stuff." He had one of the most dangerous jobs possible in the 1940s—test pilot.

Harold's days were spent in untested, untried aircraft, determining whether the nuts and bolts held together. He then reported his findings to the manufacturer before production on the aircraft could commence. Harold could have lost his life on multiple occasions, but each time God protected him. He would simply shrug, smile, and say, "It wasn't my time yet."

Harold and Lea, Priscilla's mother, loved each other intensely and passionately. After getting married in 1942, they decided to start a family. By September 1948, they lived in Torrance, California, with four children, all under five years old.

As 1948 came to a close, Lea unexpectedly conceived again just three months after giving birth to a little girl. This fifth addition to their family would likely have been welcome if it hadn't been so soon after giving birth to another child. Daily life seemed filled to overflowing with the children they already had.

In the early days of February 1949, Harold was performing a routine test flight off the coast of Long Beach, California, in a high-performing jet-propelled aircraft. The plane malfunctioned shortly after takeoff, crashing into the Pacific Ocean. Priscilla's father and his copilot both lost their lives. Harold was only twenty-eight years old.

Now alone, Harold's young, pregnant widow was uncertain what the future would hold. Likely immersed in grief and completely overwhelmed with the needs of her young children, Lea was convinced by friends that she could eliminate a lot of her stress by having an abortion. In other words, she could simplify her own life by ending her baby's.

In late February, just weeks after her husband's death, Lea took a weeklong trip to San Diego—near the border with Mexico. Lea visited friends while her grandparents back home cared for her four young children.

She also visited an abortionist in Mexico.

The abortion procedure Lea had is known as a D&C (dilation and curettage): A doctor dilates the cervix manually with specialized instruments, then uses a sharp curette to scrape the uterus of its contents. This procedure is sometimes done after women miscarry, to ensure that the uterus is empty and thus prevent the risk of infection. In this case, however, the intent was to end the human life growing inside Lea.

The doctor reported that the procedure was a success, which was seemingly confirmed by the expected vaginal bleeding afterward.

When Lea returned to Torrance, her grandmother noted in her diary that she looked good and that she was tanned. As far as everyone knew, Lea was no longer pregnant and probably feeling a sense of relief, having eliminated the emotional, physical, and financial demands of another child.

About a month later, Lea learned that the abortion attempt was only partially successful. It turned out that Lea had been carrying twins, and one of them survived the procedure. She entered her second trimester of pregnancy with a due date around the end of August. Imagine Lea's shock: another baby in diapers! *Two* children barely a year apart! Her grandmother remarked in her diary that when Lea heard the news, she "took it standing up."

Priscilla was born full term on August 28, 1949, in Torrance, California—the fifth child in the family, with a grieving young widow for a mother. What would the future hold? With no job and five children to support, Lea's future did not look promising. Within one year of Harold's death, however, friends of Lea's mother arranged a blind date for Lea with a man they felt would be a good catch—a doctor we'll call Walter.

It wasn't long before Walter knew he was crazy about Lea.

He loved her kids, too. Walter proposed, and later they made the decision for him to adopt all five children. Sadly, when Harold's parents learned that Walter was going to adopt the children and have their names legally changed, they cut off their relationship with Lea and the children. Somehow (Priscilla doesn't know all the details), Lea and Walter decided that all the loving emotions and fun memories made with Harold, both as a father and as a husband, would be packed away, never to be discussed again. The older children were forced into silence, which surely must have confused them. *Why couldn't they talk about their daddy?*

Lea and Walter didn't grasp the impact this would have on the older children, who were still hurting, nor on the younger ones, who had few memories of their father yet sensed the grief and confusion of everyone around them.

The new family welcomed a sixth baby in 1951. Walter provided well for his family and gave the kids a wonderful childhood. Like most children of Priscilla's generation, the kids did what their parents told them. Their parents did not tolerate any "monkey business," she says, and the children were "good little soldiers."

Despite all that obedience, the pain of the children's unmet emotional needs ran deep. Priscilla in particular lacked a healthy sense of self, and she began to act out. Priscilla says she longed to be loved, to be held, and to believe she was wanted, yet that longing was never satisfied. As a young woman, off at college and away from the restrictions of home life, Priscilla thought she could manage those feelings, but her emotional needs drove her to make risky decisions. Without goals, without a sense of purpose, and without an internal moral code, she was aimless and undisciplined, making choices she would later regret.

REPEATING THE PATTERN

Priscilla's unfulfilled longings led to sexual relationships, which led to an unplanned pregnancy at age nineteen. Terrified and with no idea what to do, she called her mother. Mom knew exactly what needed to be done. There was no discussion. The decision was made for her. Thanks to the influence of her adoptive father and his medical colleagues, the hospital board approved an abortion.

Feeling coerced, yet convinced she had no choice, Priscilla had a D&C (the same procedure used for her mother's abortion attempt nineteen years earlier). The abortion took place under general anesthesia, so she has no memory of it. She stayed one night in the hospital and was then sent home. In short order, her mother returned her to college, where Priscilla now had another trauma to keep locked away. An already wounded child, now a young woman, Priscilla was even more broken after the coerced abortion. The once "good little soldier" was struggling and lost.

A few months later, she learned that one of her sisters also had an abortion, a saline procedure, while in college. When Priscilla and her mother went to the airport together to welcome the sister home from college, as mother and daughter walked toward the terminal from the parking lot, Lea turned to Priscilla and spoke in a very calm and matter-of-fact tone: "By the way, I tried to have you aborted."

Priscilla's heart froze. "What?"

"I tried to have you aborted."

The world stood still while Priscilla's mind spun. Stunned and shocked, she felt a stabbing pain in her gut. Her mother hadn't wanted her to be born? What was the good little soldier supposed to say to this news? Since she didn't know, she didn't say anything.

Like her mom, nineteen years earlier, was she supposed to take this "standing up" and just move forward?

As the revelation sank in, many of the questions Priscilla had while growing up started to make sense. Why did she feel unwanted and unloved as a child? Why was her mom so cold and distant? Why did she feel so alone? Why did she have so many sad memories—despite a childhood that from the outside appeared ideal? Perhaps this explained why her mother was unable to demonstrate affection or love, to Priscilla in particular. What's more, she came to understand why directing her own daughter to have an abortion was an easy decision for Lea.

Priscilla was baffled as to why her mother chose that moment to reveal her secret. Since both Priscilla and her sister had now experienced abortion, perhaps Lea now felt free to speak of a decision made nineteen years earlier. But that lone bit of information was all Priscilla got. Nothing more.

Lea's attempt to abort her confused Priscilla. How could her mother make such a choice? She'd already had four babies, so she understood the value of children and what it meant to have a family. Did the pain and anger of losing her beloved husband make her rationalize what she was about to do? Was she influenced by friends and family members? Priscilla never felt free to discuss the subject with her mother.

Six years later, when Priscilla was twenty-five, she again found herself pregnant. Her boyfriend, Charles, a law student pursuing his dream career, pressured her to resolve this "little mistake" they had made. Charles made all the arrangements for an abortion and committed to paying for it. Priscilla was reluctant, but she loved Charles and didn't want to disappoint him, nor did she want to lose the man she thought she might one day marry. Although Priscilla did not want an abortion, she eventually agreed.

This time, however, she was awake—and frightened—throughout the procedure. The doctor hardly said a word to her and didn't seem to care whether she was ready for the procedure. When the vacuum aspiration machine began making its loud, awful sound, Priscilla realized she was nothing more than a piece of meat, her child a target for the machine's cannula.

When the procedure was complete, Priscilla was left empty and horrified by the experience. She couldn't stop grieving about it—how cold and blind the procedure had been, how alone and unprepared she had felt.

Charles attempted to help her through this difficult time. He arranged for her to meet with the young director of another abortion clinic. Priscilla hoped the woman could educate her about the process *post-procedure*, as the director often did with women *before* their abortions. She hoped that their meeting would help her get to the other side of her darkness. As the director and Priscilla talked, Priscilla was impressed with the level of support offered to the clinic's patients. The director took note of Priscilla's positive response and introduced her to another clinic director. They both took a liking to her.

When they offered Priscilla a job, the idea struck her as strangely compelling. It wasn't so much that she *wanted* to work there; she felt she *had* to. She did not yet understand how that sense of compulsion might be coming from the trauma of her past—a past that affected everything about who she was, how others saw her, and what motivated and drove her. So when the clinic offered her the job, she thought it was a chance to address this turbulent place inside her, as though doing the good work of helping women through their abortions would somehow pour salve on her own emotional wounds and fill the void within that she didn't yet know could be addressed only by a Savior.

But the idea that this job would provide a way for her to contribute to a good cause unraveled pretty quickly.

The first thing she noticed in the clinic was how the workers were instructed to be very careful to choose words that downplayed or distracted from the stark truth. It wasn't a *baby*. It was a *mass*, or *remains*, or *products of conception*. They lied, telling the women the procedure wasn't painful when it was, in fact, very painful—something Priscilla knew from her own abortion as well as from holding the hands of women during their abortions. She could see from the pain etched in their expressions that the procedure hurt terribly. The clinic told their potential clients that recovery would be a breeze. In fact, it was bloody and terrifying. And the truth they absolutely kept hidden was that some women never recovered. Certainly nothing was said about the emotional toll—which could be the worst suffering of all.

Images of body parts gathered in Priscilla's memory, refusing to dissipate. And as all these things piled up, a battle began to wage about how she was complicit in the lies being spoken and enacted.

The house of cards she'd built came tumbling down one day when she was one of two workers addressing some pregnant women who had questions about abortion.

One young woman raised her hand.

"Yes?" Priscilla said, giving her the floor.

She had an earnest look on her face. "Is abortion killing?" she asked.

The room went silent and cold. Priscilla's stomach leaped to her throat. This was a new question. She didn't know how to respond, so she turned to her coworker, a director, for the answer.

"Well, is it killing when you swat a fly?" the director asked. "Because that's the size of what it is."

The director's response slammed into Priscilla and nearly broke her. The director hadn't truly listened to this young woman's heart. She hadn't paid enough attention to the look in her eyes to understand that she was fighting for a reason to let her baby live. The director should have seen that this woman was wrestling with something much larger than a merely clinical procedure and referred her to someone who could address the real issue. Instead, "the director reduced the abortion procedure to nothing more than a fly swatter, and the life inside her to an unwanted bug."

By this point, Priscilla had no illusion that the reason behind everything the clinic did was to help women. It was clearly to make money. She didn't want to be a part of it anymore. But she felt stuck. Glued to the job she no longer wanted.

Not long after that, Priscilla was driving to work one day when a large car blew through the intersection she was crossing in her little VW. The big car T-boned hers, crushing her car as well as her neck.

During the weeks of recuperation that followed, having just escaped death, Priscilla was no longer the same young woman. She began to question everything about her life—who she was, what she was doing, where she was going, and her place in the world.

A former classmate reminded her that their professor had offered them a paid internship in Alaska, working toward a master's degree in health administration. Alaska was far from her home, but far seemed to be exactly what she needed. So she took it.

Sometime after moving to Alaska, Priscilla was visiting a neighbor one afternoon when she noticed stacks of Christian literature on the woman's table. Her curiosity piqued, she began to flip through them and was drawn to the idea of having the peace of the Holy Spirit. Over time, her neighbor proved to be an amazing and graceful witness. Many months passed, and then one day, as an unwed mom of a four-month-old, she felt the truth of the gospel wash over her. She knew she needed a Savior. That's what she wanted and needed more than anything. *Please, God, save me from me*, she prayed. And then she gave her heart to Jesus.

Almost forty years passed.

A TURNING POINT

In 2015 Priscilla participated in a ministry designed to help women heal from past abortions. She experienced some significant healing, but something deeper still remained unresolved.

Five years later Priscilla discovered ASN and found herself trying to better understand her mother's abortion experience. She wondered how her mother had first reacted to the news that her abortion attempt had failed. Was she devastated? Dismayed? Angry? Or was she perhaps relieved? Did she think her baby—Priscilla— was a miracle, and that God had overridden her plan?

What kinds of questions must have flooded her mother's heart? Had she wondered whether she could love all her children after the loss of her dear Harold—the one who had defined her life, who had been the sunshine in her day? Was her grief-stricken, depressed state something she could not shake? Even more, did she wonder, *How did this baby survive the D&C?* Now, as a mature woman of faith, Priscilla was so much better equipped to see her mother through a lens of mercy.

When I, the founder of ASN, heard Priscilla's story, I suggested that she get in touch with Abby Johnson, who runs a ministry called And Then There Were None that brings healing to people who spent time in the abortion industry. At first Priscilla thought that wasn't necessary, because many years had passed since she'd been in the industry. But she had seen *Unplanned*—the 2019 movie based on Abby's story—and was deeply impressed with her. People of Abby's courage and conviction don't come around very often, so Priscilla decided to give the ministry a chance.

Priscilla attended one of Abby's healing retreats, and on the ministry's website, AbortionWorker.com, Priscilla wrote about her experience:

"Abby instructed us to add up, as best we could, the number of deaths that happened while working at our clinics. When I was done, the number was 7,000. I contributed to 7,000 deaths. The weight of the number pushes one to their knees in confession and repentance, as it did me—and that is the only place healing can begin.

"Judging by how I feel now—truly forgiven for what I had done, I had no idea how much I needed to come to the foot of the throne of God by the blood of his son, Jesus. Healing is a journey and I can feel my feet firmly on that road, growing lighter every day."

Today, as Priscilla thinks about how God's hand sheltered her little body and protected her from the abortionist's instrument of death, she marvels. Had she not survived the abortion attempt, she would not be the mother of three adult children, grandmother of eleven, and great-grandmother of two. She would not be a sister, aunt, coworker, friend, prayer partner, or wife.

Although it took many years to find Him, Priscilla is profoundly grateful to now live under God's mercy every day. It has been through her repentance, God's forgiveness, and growth in her faith that God has mercifully restored her soul and renewed her mind.

Priscilla would like to leave us with these words:

Living daily with Christ, I finally found what I was always longing for: a connection with my loving Creator. What was meant for evil, God will use for good. My life is proof of that truth. My life has been rich and productive, my heart full of the love of God. I continue daily under construction of my faith and the restoration of my soul. We are His creation, and there is no one more grateful to be with Him than this broken, hurting, traumatized child, who can now testify to His lovingkindness with a renewed life and live out my life in the light of His love, loving others and glorifying Him.

4

THE BROKEN CHAIN: MICHELLE'S STORY

Michelle with her birth mother, Tracy

MICHELLE'S TINY HEART FIRST STARTED BEATING inside her mother's womb in the summer of 1964. But like all of us, Michelle's story really began with her parents' stories—with events she didn't learn about until she was seventeen. I think Michelle would agree that she is still trying to make peace with those events several decades later. And that's okay. Sometimes we have to let a story's influences reveal themselves in their own good time.

So *I'm* not going to tell you Michelle's story about surviving abortion—at least not from its beginning. Instead, I'll let Michelle herself describe what she knew and experienced before she ever heard her origin story.

ALWAYS ON THE MOVE

Growing up, I often felt I had no value. From my earliest memories, my four siblings and I were like hot potatoes—passed back and forth between our parents (who were no longer together), grandparents, and other relatives. Sometimes we were kept together, sometimes not.

I recall a day when we five kids piled into a van. We were moving again, this time to Ogden, Utah, with the man I understood to be my dad. His name was Mark, and he was taking us to live with his mom. She was a single mother of nine, with three children still at home who were not much older than us. I was in kindergarten at the time, and we had all been staying with our mother's parents in Claremore, Oklahoma. Living with grandparents on either side of the family, while not even close to perfect, was far better for us than living with our parents.

By the time school started up again, Mark had found a house to rent, so we left Grandma's house to live with him. We were home alone most of the time while he was out installing carpet. While living in Utah, eating a family meal together was even more rare than having an adult around. We learned early on how to fend for ourselves, making do with whatever we could find. We ate many "Miracle Whip on bread" meals, along with jars of baby food. (We learned later that Mark had found them at the site of a train wreck.)

My first-grade teacher was a sweet and kind lady who showed genuine concern for me, though at first I thought she was unhappy with me. Back then I suffered from terrible eczema, to the point that my hands and arms would bleed. It must have been evident to her that there was severe neglect at home. She told me on several occasions that I should ask my parents to get some lotion for me. I was a compliant child and wanted to do what she asked, but I didn't know how to get lotion on my own. One morning I arrived at class thinking

I was going to be in trouble because I still didn't have the lotion. She surprised me with a bottle she had bought just for me. This small act of kindness made me feel loved and valued.

Later in the year, she assigned us a class project to create our own cards for Mother's Day. I looked around the room at all the other children. They were eager to begin, and I thought, Why do they have moms and I don't? *It had been so long since I had seen or talked to my mother that I had nearly forgotten who she was.*

Then one day, as the five of us siblings were passing a restaurant on our way to school, two women pulled us inside. My two older siblings recognized one of the women as our mother right away. Her name was Tracy, and the other woman, we were told, was her friend Gail. That very day, the two of them flew us all to Detroit, Michigan, where Mom immediately left us with Gail so she could go prepare a place for us to hide at a nearby horse racing track. At Gail's place, to my delight, I met a sister I didn't know I had. Her name was Charlie Joe. She was a little over a year old and one of the cutest things I had ever seen in my life.

Mark, the man I thought was our father, was never again a part of our lives.

Rick, our mom's current boyfriend and father to our newfound baby sister, was a jockey. Once the tack rooms were ready, they snuck us in during the dark of night. They warned us repeatedly that no one was to know we were there, and we were not to make a sound.

Rick showed no emotion and was extremely quiet, cruel, and abusive. One day, my six-year-old sister Kasi and I were sitting quietly with our backs to the door, coloring, when suddenly we felt a sting on our backs. We cried out in pain and turned to see Rick with a horse whip in his hand. He looked at us and smiled. Without speaking a word, he turned and left.

Tracy and Rick had a turbulent, on- and off-again relationship.

Many nights, we crawled out of windows to seek help from neighbors because of the violence between them. Police officers would come and go, but there was never any intervention. I might not have had a clear understanding of what "normal" was, but I knew that our current "normal" wasn't good for any of us.

We eventually moved out of the tack room. One day when I was twelve, as I sat on the floor watching Little House on the Prairie— *my favorite television show—Mom, in passing, remarked with irritation, "Why are you watching that? It isn't reality." I thought,* This is the family I want to model my life after, rather than anything like the "reality" I am living in.

By the time I was fifteen, I was in a very dark and hopeless place. Life was too painful to keep living, so I decided to end my life. I took a handful of Valium pills and went to sleep. When I awoke, I was upset to find I was still alive.

Shortly thereafter, I chose to leave home. Since I had no place else to go, I called my best friend, Sandi—a girl I met in seventh grade while staying with one of my grandmas in Lancaster, California. Sandi had befriended me even though I'd been the target of almost constant bullying and spent most of my time alone. Sandi and her mom were always good to me and took me under their protective wings. They were Christians and introduced me to Jesus. I ended up spending way more time with them in their home than I did in my own. I went to church and other events with them as often as possible.

Fortunately, when I decided to leave home at fifteen, Sandi asked her mother if I could come live with them. Her mom loved me, and she said yes. My neighborhood friends helped me gather enough money to make the trip. Sandi's mother was very strict. She required us to go to school and church, and she wouldn't allow us to wear certain clothes or watch certain movies. As a fifteen-year-old, I pretended to be bothered by all this mothering, but secretly I loved it! I knew she believed in me and saw that my life had value. Sandi's family owned and operated a janitorial cleaning company. If we were not in school, church, or an event, we worked for the family business to earn our own spending money. I stayed with Sandi's family for nearly a year and will be forever grateful for their influence on my life.

Even more moves followed. At sixteen I moved to Las Vegas, Nevada. At seventeen, I made the almost two-hundred-mile drive from Vegas to visit my mom and siblings in Hesperia, California. During this visit, my mother and I were sitting in her bedroom at her little round table, pleasantly chatting. That's when she commented: "It's a miracle that you're even alive at all."

I knew that I had been run over as a toddler. Assuming that's what her comment was about, I began to ask her for more details about the accident. She explained that one day Mark and one of my uncles decided to run an errand, but as they were pulling out, Mark felt his truck run over something. He assumed it was a toy, yet when he got out to look, he saw that his truck tire was on top of my head! I was rushed to the local hospital in critical condition. My pelvis had been crushed, my skull cracked open, and I was placed in a full-body cast.

Yet the accident did little to slow me down. My mom told me that I scooted around in my cast for months, wearing it out to the point it had to come off earlier than planned. The doctor explained to my mother that I would very likely be crippled and might never walk again. According to her, however, I walked out of the office to everyone's astonishment once the cast was off!

AN EVEN DEEPER SECRET

As seventeen-year-old Michelle listened to her mother recount this story, she assumed it explained Tracy's comment "It's a miracle that you're even alive at all." But her mother wasn't finished. She began to reminisce about her own teen years and proceeded to reveal a much deeper secret she had kept concealed for Michelle's entire life.

In 1958, fifteen-year-old Tracy met twenty-year-old Jack. They became the best of friends and had many adventures together, but after a few years they chose separate paths. In 1961, now-eighteen-year-old Tracy married Mark, who was a year or so younger than her. In rapid succession—1961, 1962, and 1963—the couple had three children.

By the summer of 1964, Tracy was feeling unhappy with her life. She called her old friend Jack and asked him to come get her in Ogden, Utah, where she was living with Mark. So Jack picked up Tracy and took her back to Las Vegas with him.

A few months later, Tracy realized she was pregnant. In an attempt to cover up her affair with Jack and the child they had created together, the couple came up with a plan: Tracy would return to Mark and make it appear that he had fathered the child. Jack handed her the keys to his red 1958 hardtop MG sports car, and off she went toward Utah. But she only made it halfway before the car broke down. Once again she called Jack, who rescued her and took her back to Vegas. It was then they learned that Mark had been observed sneaking around the house and putting sugar in the gas tank of Jack's car. Realizing that Mark must have discovered their affair, Jack and Tracy gave up on their plan to make Mark believe the child was his.

Instead, Tracy decided to seek out an abortion without telling Jack. (By this point Jack was looking forward to being a father and wanted to marry Tracy.) Yet back in 1964, abortions were illegal in most states, including Nevada. One night Tracy went out, as she often did, to a Las Vegas bar. She met up with some people who said they could help her abort the pregnancy. Tracy took them up on it and arranged a back-alley abortion. The abortionist used a coat hanger, and Tracy returned home to Jack. Bleeding profusely, she soon confessed what she'd done. Her bleeding was so heavy that they both worried she might bleed to death.

As Tracy recovered, Jack realized he was both relieved and angry. He was relieved that he wouldn't face the shame of fathering the child of another man's wife. But he was angry at Tracy for having the abortion without his knowledge or consent. Over time, Jack became so upset that he forced Tracy to leave, and she ended up returning to her husband.

After a few months passed, Tracy realized that she was still pregnant. The back-alley abortion had failed, and her pregnancy began to show. She briefly considered trying a second abortion, but she couldn't shake the thought that maybe God had intervened to save the baby. She didn't want to risk "getting in trouble with God," so she allowed the pregnancy to proceed.

Surprisingly, Michelle says, "Everyone pretended that the coming child was Mark's—even Mark."

Before the baby arrived, Mark and Tracy moved to El Monte, California. One day while Mark was at work, Tracy was at home when she began experiencing sudden and intense labor pains. Her neighbors could not speak English, but they saw her distress and called for help.

"The story my mom told me," Michelle says, "is that a police officer arrived just in time and assisted in my birth. Mine might have been the first birth he had ever attended. He was ecstatic and repeatedly proclaimed how beautiful I was."

Shortly after Michelle's birth, Tracy called Jack to tell him he had a daughter who shared his same blue eyes. It would be the last he would hear from Tracy for the next fifteen years.

Tracy and Mark moved back to Ogden. Eleven months after

delivering Michelle, Tracy gave birth to another daughter, giving them a total of five very young children. And that's when it truly began—the chaos, abuse, trauma, and neglect that Michelle described above.

I'll let Michelle pick up the story once more.

"I WAS BROKEN"

As my mother told me this story, I did not tell her I'd known since I was ten that Mark was not my biological father. One of my grandmas had let the cat out of the bag about who my real father was. You'd think it might be devastating for a ten-year-old to learn this, but for me it wasn't. Because my relationship with Mark had never been close, this knowledge gave me hope for a better father—something I desperately needed. That same grandma even arranged for me to visit my biological father, Jack. However, she insisted that I keep it a secret from my mother and everyone else except my grandma's husband. I honored her instructions and kept my relationship and visits with Jack secret for years. Spending that time with my father and his family was a dream come true, and I loved being with him more than anything in the world.

But now, at seventeen, the revelation of the secret of my mom's attempt to have me aborted had a very different impact. It was crushing. I almost fell out of my chair.

Later on, when I spoke with my grandma about my mother's attempt to end my life, I remember her being shocked. "She actually told you about it?" she asked. The first time I brought it up with my dad (Jack), he had a similar reaction and almost seemed relieved that I finally knew.

I had grown up in so much chaos and dysfunction, and my subsequent choices reinforced the adage that "broken families produce broken people." I was broken. I had no understanding of my true value.

I felt rejected, unlovable, and worthless for much of my life, and that played out in the choices I made. By age twenty, I was a single mother to an almost two-year-old child and was once again pregnant by a man I barely knew.

In my shame, I decided to marry my second baby's father. I figured that no one would know I was already pregnant before the wedding, and if the marriage didn't work out, I would just get a divorce. When I discovered that I had married an abusive and violent alcoholic, I wanted to run. I was at a crossroads and thought, I am making so many bad decisions. This is not the life or the future I want for myself and my children.

That's when my life took a dramatic turn. I decided that the safest place to run was toward God, so I chose to let Him be in charge of my decisions. In fact, I dedicated my life to God. Soon after this, my husband and I were invited to a church service where a guest speaker called us up front. He began to pray over us. Part of his prayer for me was, "Father, I see her standing in her kitchen, giving you praise for what you are doing in her husband's life." Then he said to me, "God wants you to know that He inhabits the praises of His people."

His words sent shock waves through me! Earlier that same day, I had been standing in my kitchen, washing dishes, when the Scripture that says "Give thanks in all circumstances" (1 Thessalonians 5:18) came to mind. So, with the right heart and attitude, I began to give God thanks. My prayer that day went something like Thank You, Lord, that even though my husband got drunk, broke his arm in a fight, and lost his job, and we will be losing our health insurance with a baby coming, Your Word says all things work together for good for those who love You and are called according to Your purpose (Romans 8:28).

That church service was transformational for me because I began to understand God's great love for me. I finally began to understand my true worth. God saw me there in my kitchen, and He touched my heart with His very presence. I wept many tears—tears of thankfulness for the mercy, grace, love, and goodness that He poured into my soul, into my brokenness. Encountering Christ and His healing shattered my once-impenetrable shell. My fear and shame were replaced with confidence and a calling to boldly speak truth to those around me.

God not only began to transform my life, but He did a quick and powerful work in my husband's life as well. With a broken arm and no job or money, he had lots of time for Bible study! God gave me a new man, and he has been walking with the Lord ever since.

I went on to bear seven children in all. I had a very large family like my mother, but thanks to an amazing relationship with Jesus Christ, my family's generational pattern of abuse and chaos ended with me. My husband and I have provided a home for our children filled with love, perseverance, and commitment to Christ. And that home blessed not only our own children but also my siblings and many other precious souls God entrusted to our care for a season.

Here I am, more than thirty-five years of marriage later, with ten children (my husband had three of his own, so we have a blended family), twenty-one grandchildren, and three great-grandchildren. Generational patterns have been broken, and every one of these lives is a beautiful gift! And Jesus is still at work, shaping who I am today as a sister, wife, mother, grandmother, daughter, advocate, and friend.

SURVIVOR'S GUILT

As I've come to know Michelle, one of the most amazing outcomes to me is how God has redeemed Michelle's relationship with her mother, Tracy. Today, though they live hundreds of miles apart, they speak frequently, and Michelle supports her in many practical and tangible ways. Michelle is an ongoing source of comfort to her mother. And to think that, at one time, Tracy resorted to a coat hanger to rid herself of Michelle's existence!

Michelle says one particular aspect of her story continues to cause her to struggle: "I know in my head that I'm not personally responsible for legalized abortion, but I struggle with feeling like my existence caused my mother's attempt to abort me with a coat hanger, and that this—back-alley, coat-hanger abortions—is what ultimately led to legalizing abortion." She wrestles with feelings of guilt for being a reminder of coat-hanger abortions, since she realizes that the horrible dangers of that method are what helped convince many people to support legalized abortion.

I know full well that Michelle is not to blame, but I also understand where she is coming from. One of the ugliest symbols in the long battle over abortion is the coat hanger. For years, proponents of legalized abortion wielded placards with images of bloodied hangers as evidence that women in crisis pregnancies were doomed to suffer at the hands of the medically unqualified. *Stop the back-alley butchering of our women*, they read. *Legalize abortion! Make it safe. Make it legal.* And with the passage of *Roe v. Wade*, abortion proponents won the day.

Yet making abortion *legal* didn't actually make it *safe*. As Joseph Dellapenna, author of *Dispelling the Myths of Abortion History*, perhaps the most definitive work on the topic, has written: "The data suggest that there have been as many maternal deaths in the United States annually from legal abortions (estimates range from 15 to 35 per year) as there were maternal deaths from illegal abortions in the years immediately before *Roe v. Wade* was decided."[1]

Despite those numbers, Michelle's survivor's guilt is still a heavy load. It's difficult to release a burden you've carried for decades. Hard, but not impossible. Michelle has spent a long time surrendering that false guilt to the Lord and seeking His healing. She understands that healing is a process and trusts God to complete that process in her with the help of the Holy Spirit.

So now, when Michelle sees an image of a coat hanger, she chooses to view her story as still in the making. She sees her life as God's victory over her mother's misguided decision to abort. Michelle believes, as do I, that had abortion been legal, there's a much greater chance that she would not have survived. The story of her spiritual redemption would be gone. The impact of her love and care for her siblings—gone. The lives of her own children and grandchildren—gone. Breaking the chains of generational abuse—gone.

That lifetime of experience gives Michelle the confidence to speak powerful words of hope and life to others, so I'll give her the last word:

When our culture shakes a coat hanger in contempt, I see my life, my family, and future generations to come. Had God's hand not protected my life and brought restoration to my heart, none of this would have been possible. He is the God of the impossible and a worker of miracles. If I can overcome all that I have through Christ, then you can too!

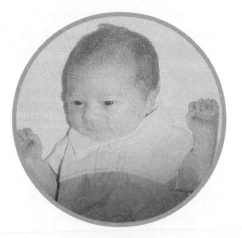

5

THE CHRISTMAS GIFT: JAMES'S STORY

James as an infant

JAMES WAS A CHRISTMAS GIFT TO HIS PARENTS— a gift they almost didn't receive. When James's mother became pregnant in 1976, her doctor determined she had a condition that would put her life at risk if she continued the pregnancy. The doctor also warned the couple that their baby would likely not survive. He put considerable pressure on James's mother to abort, both for the sake of her own health and to prevent the baby from suffering.

The couple already had six children at the time, all from previous marriages. Though not eager to abort, they chose to follow the doctor's advice and proceeded with a saline-solution procedure. On the day of James's mother's abortion, however, the couple were confused when nothing about her body's response to the procedure seemed to progress the way the doctor had described. They were eventually sent home with the understanding that the abortion was complete.

A few months passed, and the couple realized that James's mother was still pregnant. At this point they felt that since they'd tried abortion once and for some reason the baby had survived, maybe the child was meant to live.

James was born on Christmas Day and was welcomed with loving arms into a grateful family. His parents decided that no good would ever come from telling James the story of the abortion attempt, so they kept it as their secret. They were relieved that he appeared to be a healthy baby and had suffered no ill effects from the saline procedure. Only later, as he matured, did they discover that James had an unusual deficiency related to the sensitivity of his skin—a condition that continues to this day. This lack of sensitivity means that James can grab something hot and burn himself rather badly without realizing that he is damaging his skin. There is no medical proof that this condition was caused by the saline-abortion attempt, but James's parents believe the two are related.

When James was five years old, his parents divorced and eventually remarried other people. To the credit of his mother and father, both maintained a healthy and loving relationship with him. Young James lived primarily with his mother and stepfather, visiting his father on weekends, holidays, and vacations. James enjoyed the sense of family and connection they all shared, and he and his siblings still stay in touch.

James eventually married Phyllis, yet his parents still kept secret the circumstances surrounding his birth. But secrets, it seems, often have a way of coming to light.

A MYSTERIOUS CONDITION

James and Phyllis were out shopping one day when he heard someone call his name. Yet when James turned toward the voice, he did not recognize the man's jubilant face.

"James!" the stranger exclaimed. "Man, it's been forever! How are you?" Clearly the man knew James. He quickly launched into a trip down memory lane, mentioning James's dad and all the fun they had fishing, swimming, and boating on the lake when they were younger. Now in his thirties, James was totally clueless about this stranger and embarrassed that he didn't recognize him. They clearly shared a past, however, so James played along. James must have faked it well enough, since the man didn't seem to notice. And the more they talked, the more it became frighteningly clear to James that he'd known this man for more than twenty-five years!

This encounter, along with some other extremely alarming memory lapses, sent James to his doctor, accompanied by Phyllis. Following a series of tests, James learned that he had frontal lobe epilepsy. This complex and mysterious condition can manifest in various ways; it turns out that James was unaware of the seizures that caused scar tissue to form in his frontal lobe. This scar tissue, in turn, led to his episodic memory loss. The causes of frontal lobe epilepsy range from simple genetics to head trauma that can cause lesions in the frontal lobe of the brain. But in James's case, the doctors could not pinpoint the cause.

James and Phyllis embarked on what has become a lifelong journey of managing his condition. This includes the question of how to handle precious memories.

"One day I realized I had no idea what our wedding day was like," James says. "I knew when it was. I knew where it was, who had performed it, who had been my best man, and things like that. We had pictures and mementos that told all that. But I couldn't recall the day at all as *my* wedding. It could've been anyone's wedding. And then, as I kept thinking, I realized that it was the same for any kind of college experience, any kind of high school experience, anything. And to this day, I really don't know what it is I don't remember until it comes up and I realize I'm blank on it."

SLIP OF THE TONGUE

James and Phyllis cope with his memory loss by recounting stories of his life as a way to help him own and treasure his past. But frontal lobe epilepsy wasn't the only revelation James had in his early thirties. The couple learned that James's father (who was single at the time) required heart surgery followed by an extended period of recuperation. James and Phyllis agreed it would be best if his father stayed with them for a time.

When heading out the door one day to run a quick errand, James's father casually said, "All right. I'll see you guys a little later." Then, in a tone of voice clearly meant to be one of affection, he added, "Do you know you're my favorite little abortion?"

James and Phyllis exchanged shocked and confused expressions. James asked his father the obvious question.

"What do you mean by that?"

His father stopped in his tracks. He hesitated for a moment, slowly turned around, looked directly into his son's searching eyes, and said, "Well, I guess now is as good a time as any to tell you."

James gulped as his dad stepped back inside the house. That's when James finally heard the story of the doctor's frightening diagnosis, the pressure on his parents to abort, their reluctant decision to accept the doctor's advice, and the subsequent failure of that abortion.

James was stunned. He'd never heard of a baby surviving an abortion under any circumstances. As he tried to wrap his mind around the news, his thoughts and emotions collided in a mix of horror, hurt, relief, and disbelief.

My parents tried to abort me, even though they didn't want to? I was poisoned in the womb with my parents' cooperation, yet I inexplicably survived? My parents were later grateful and relieved that I survived? I was kept in the dark about the details of my birth for more than thirty years?

"It was like finding out that unicorns are real," James says, "and at the same time learning I'd had my horn removed!"

At the moment, James felt sure of only one thing—his father's love. He could see the love in his father's eyes. He could hear the gratitude in his father's voice. And as odd—bizarre, even—as it was to be called "my favorite little abortion," there was no mistaking that his father's slip of the tongue was meant as a term of endearment. Naturally, James had lots of questions. His father, in turn, was patient and eager to answer every one that he could.

There was one question, though, that neither James's father nor his doctor could answer: Was the attempted abortion responsible for James's frontal lobe epilepsy? They simply didn't know.

James wanted to discuss the abortion attempt with his mother as well, but he was hesitant. He thought it would be a painful subject for her, and he was right. When James did finally broach the subject, his mother was clearly uncomfortable. She spoke of experiencing guilt and shame over their decision to take the doctor's advice—complicated by the fact that when she did, in fact, carry James to term, neither she nor he suffered any of the ill effects the doctor had predicted. She'd jeopardized the life of her child for nothing, and she deeply regretted it. As in the conversation with his dad, James walked away assured of his mother's love. And to avoid causing additional pain, James never mentioned it to his mother again.

NOT ALONE

A few years ago, James happened across a Facebook ad for ASN. He was amazed to discover that he wasn't the only abortion survivor out there—that there were more of us. *How many others are there who've had an experience like mine?* he wondered. *How could we help and encourage one another?* James decided to find out, so he contacted ASN and began attending some of our online events.

"What a privilege just to be able to connect with others," James said, "even if it's just via social media, through a private group that only other survivors can attend. To be able to just talk to each other, encourage each other, has been really powerful and encouraging. It's rewarding to share something so unique. Of course, because of my memory loss, I don't have a lot of experiential memories to share. So while I can know that a certain event happened, I don't necessarily remember experiencing that event. This limits my participation. But even so, I get to hear the experiences of all these other people and be so appreciative of what God has brought about in my own life. Every one of their stories is so different. And mine is certainly unique.

"Hearing others' stories, I've been moved with a great deal of gratitude because I understand why so many survivors grew up wondering if they were loved or wanted, or feeling like they didn't belong. Because my parents both wanted me and celebrated my survival, I grew up knowing I was loved and belonged to my family—even in spite of the complicated family tree with multiple divorces and remarriages."

James and Phyllis are today the proud parents of three sons, all of them via adoption. Because every child's story is so important, James says, he already makes a habit of telling his oldest son about the day he was born.

"I tell him how we, as his chosen mother and father, traveled to the hospital to see him right away—and how, when he was ready to be discharged, we took him to a hotel where we stayed for a couple of weeks until the adoption papers could be finalized. He loves that story, and I love telling him. Because of my condition, I'm no longer sure if I actually remember those events or if I simply remember telling him about them again and again, but that doesn't matter. What matters is that he knows we wanted him, chose him, and love him. Now our second son is just old enough to begin that same tradition, and we'll do the same for our youngest."

Making sure that his sons know their stories isn't James's greatest priority, however. "My true identity," he says, "is bound in Christ. He redeemed me as a fairly young man and purchased me with a price, and I have committed my life to Him for a long time now. I approach [fatherhood] with the desire to see [my sons] know Christ, to see them grow in Him, to see them know His words, and to see them grow in godliness. And so with that as my priority—and all the more so because of my own track record of how I lived life as a young man and how I lived life as a young adult—my focus is on putting Christ in front of them and seeing them raised in His image and in His Word. They will always know that they belong, that they are loved, and that their life is a gift."

I love how James, a Christmas Day gift to his parents, passes along to his sons the assurance that their lives are also gifts. Every child is a gift!

6

PROTECTED FOR A PURPOSE: MICAELLA'S STORY

Micaella

FOR HER FIRST SIX YEARS OF LIFE, Micaella lived in foster homes in Illinois with her birth brother, Carlos, who was nearly two years older. For many years her early life remained a mystery. As often happens in the foster care system, she and Carlos bounced from home to home. Micaella can't recall very much about them, but she can count more than thirty different homes where they stayed.

When Mica (her nickname) was six and Carlos was eight, the siblings were told they were about to meet some prospective adoptive parents. As they anxiously awaited the arrival of a potential new mother and father, her brother gave her instructions.

"Don't smile too much," he warned, "and don't be nasty or mean."

Mica always viewed Carlos as her protector. He often slept on the floor in the hallway outside her bedroom door to help keep her safe. For as long as she could remember, Mica desperately wanted them to have a mother and father of their very own, so she promised to follow his instructions to be on her very best behavior. Besides, any ideas he had to get them out of the horrible foster home they were living in were good by her. The cigarette lighter burns on her back told the story of the abuse and hate they endured.

After school each day, Mica watched with envy as her class-mates ran outside to their waiting parents. Some parents even joined their children on the playground to push them on swings or encourage them as they climbed the monkey bars. Mica ached with longing as she watched friends leap into the open arms of their trusted parents. She sometimes pretended to wait for her own parents, but when it came time to walk home to her reality, Mica's sadness settled back in.

But this day was different. This was the day she and Carlos met a couple who were actually interested in becoming their parents, and this was the day that Mica took all Carlos's advice. To her absolute delight, Mica soon found herself sitting at a table for her first meal in her new home with her new parents—her protective older brother by her side. When her new mother placed a plate of delicious-looking food in front of her, she could only stare, amazed. There was real meat on her plate!

In their previous home, the siblings were used to eating a porridge-like substance—a concoction so thick that Mica and Carlos often used their spoons to shape it into all kinds of inter-esting figures. Anything to distract them from the foul taste of the stuff! Now, as she sampled the yummy food she'd been served, Mica marveled at the spread before her. Fresh fruit. Colorful vege-tables. *Could it get any better than this?*

As Mica was about to discover, yes, it could. The adoptive couple, who had no other children, were delighted to expand their family. They were eager to lavish wonderful gifts on Mica and Carlos and to call them their children. Mica could scarcely believe all the clean clothes that actually fit well, the rooms of their very own, the story times and games and fun and laughter and hugs—plus ice cream!—that came with the package. It seemed too good to be true. But, sure enough, it was true. Her new parents were truly kind and loving people.

One Sunday they dressed up in their nicest clothes and headed off to church. After everyone sang together, they all bowed their heads as the man up front started talking about someone. More accurately, the man was talking *to* someone. Mica began to cry. When the prayer was over, Mica's mother noticed her tears.

"Oh, sweetheart, what's wrong?" she asked Mica. "Why are you upset?" Her mother then looked anxiously at her husband. "Maybe we've brought them too soon. This is too much for her."

Mica saw that her mother was worried—that she thought Mica's tears were sad tears. "I'm not sad," Mica said. "It's just that I *know* Him. I know the person he was talking to. He's been with me my whole life."

Years later, Mica still remembers that moment well. She recalls trying, but not having the words, to explain that all her life she'd felt the presence of One who, much like her brother, was her protector. She didn't know His name. She knew nothing else about Him except that His presence was always with her, looking out for her. She remembers sitting on an ottoman when she was very little and sensing that she was not alone—that there was someone else in the room with her. She could not see anyone, yet the comforting presence was as real as the floor beneath her feet. And now, in this place—this church—she could again feel His presence and was overcome with joy when the pastor led the congregation in speaking to Him.

SHROUDED IN MYSTERY

Mica's story leaves me in awe of the mystery of God. How is it that this little girl, raised in foster homes full of fear and hate and abuse, had a personal knowledge of her loving heavenly Father? And yet she did. So much so that she recognized His presence in a house of worship.

Mica's early years were indeed shrouded in mystery. When she and Carlos were adopted in 1985, Carlos came with a birth certificate that gave his name, the date of his birth, and the specifics of his weight and length. Not Mica. Her age was an estimate— approximately six years old at the time of the adoption—since she had no official birth certificate. Instead, she had only a certificate of live birth stamped with the year of the adoption. No details, not even a birthday. Somewhere along the way, someone randomly assigned her one.

The new parents inquired about the siblings' pasts at the time of the adoption, but there were few explanations about whom or where they'd come from. As Mica grew, it was clear she had a number of serious health issues, including a deformed heart, sensitive lungs, a compromised immune system, and a host of allergies. She and her parents often heard doctors indicate that Mica's ailments likely stemmed from a "traumatic birth," but they didn't know—or couldn't say—exactly what that trauma was.

Mica always wanted to know her origin story, wanted to better understand why she and her brother never knew their biological parents. Had they been killed in an accident? Had they been married? Were she and Carlos unwanted? Abandoned? And if so, why?

Her curiosity didn't fade with age. Mica kept on wondering through her grade school and high school years, always feeling incomplete. Once she was an adult, she made numerous requests to access the files from her childhood. "Those records are sealed," she was told again and again. For years she tried, unsuccessfully, to get the records released.

At age thirty-five and now with two children of her own, Mica again attempted to see her adoption file. This time she heard a compassionate voice on the other end of the line: "I'm so sorry, but your records are sealed."

"I realize that," Mica replied. "But the reason I really need to know is for the health of my two children. I suffer from a number of medical issues, including heart, lung, spine, and immune system conditions. I'm worried about my children and whether my conditions are hereditary. I worry that they might struggle with the same conditions. Please, is there anything you can tell me?"

There was a pause. "May I call you back on my personal time?" the social worker asked. Mica eagerly agreed, hopeful for some information at last. The worker finally called back after the office had closed.

"I'll tell you what few details are in your file," she said, "though I have to warn you, it's not much."

Mica's heart was pounding, and she realized she was holding her breath. She let it out, paused, then took a slow, deep breath as the social worker began.

Mica's birth mother, she was told, arrived at an abortion clinic along with her nearly two-year-old son, Carlos. The mother, likely near the end of her second trimester, underwent an abortion, yet somehow the tiny baby survived and was delivered alive. Her mother left the clinic soon after, leaving behind both her premature daughter and, astonishingly, Carlos. Sometime later (the records are unclear about how much time passed) the clinic workers handed the children over to a local hospital. From there the siblings entered the foster care system until they were adopted six years later.

At last Mica had an explanation for what her doctors suspected was a "traumatic birth." She had survived her own abortion, violently emerging from her mother's body approximately three months premature. Her heart, lungs, spine, and immune system were all compromised.

Mica thanked the kind social worker and hung up.

Her first emotion was relief. She thanked God that her health issues weren't hereditary. They were caused instead by the trauma associated with her birth—either the abortion itself or by her premature arrival.

Despite her initial relief, this information was still a lot to process. Until now, she'd lived with a sense of mystery surrounding her beginnings. Now her story had new words to describe it.

Abortion.

Abandoned.

These new words were harsh and ugly.

My own mother—the one person who should have protected me—had tried to abort me instead? And then, when I survived the attempt, my mother had not only abandoned her newborn baby—not knowing if I would live or die—but abandoned her toddler son as well?

At first this new information, rather than providing answers, simply gave her more questions: How old was her mother at the time? What were her circumstances? Was she alone, poor, desperate, in danger? What would motivate a woman to abandon not one child, but two? Where had she gone? Did she ever marry and have more children? Was she still alive? Did she ever wonder what happened to Mica and Carlos? Did she ever regret her actions?

Mica was at a crossroads. She had choices to make. How would she respond? How would this new information affect her identity, her worth, her purpose? Would she continue searching for more details or let it rest?

Mica credits her heavenly Father, whose presence has been with her since childhood, for the growth she has experienced since that day. Mica could choose to look at her past and see a child selected by her own mother to die, or she could choose to see a child selected by God to be spared. She could view herself as a victim or as a survivor. She could see herself as abandoned or as chosen for adoption. She could focus on those first six horrible years in foster care or on the blessing of a protective big brother and, ultimately, the loving parents who chose her and have lavished her with love for the last twenty-nine years.

Mica chose Isaiah 54:17 as her theme verse: "No weapon that is fashioned against you shall succeed." The enemy had indeed unleashed the weapons of abortion, abandonment, and abuse against her, but God was her protector, and He saw to it that not one of those weapons succeeded.

She took stock of her life and the choices she had made thus far. She spent years working in foster homes and youth camps, doing what she could to improve the lives of children who, like her, were forced to navigate the foster care system. She invested herself in these children, imparting messages of value and worth and hope and compassion.

Now that she knew a fragment of her birth mother's story, she wanted to find her so that she could impart those same messages to her. Instead of bitterness or resentment, Mica felt compassion for her birth mother. She wanted to tell her face-to-face: "I forgive you."

Armed with this new motivation, Mica tracked down every lead she could find. In November 2020, Mica finally learned her mother's name and location, only to discover that she had died eight months earlier in March 2020.

While the enemy might have fashioned her birth mother's death as a weapon, it did not succeed. As a result of her research, Mica discovered ASN, and today she serves as a tremendous encourager and friend to many other abortion survivors. Mica proclaims to her fellow survivors, "I know that I am loved. You, too, are loved, and you have a purpose in this world. You've been chosen."

Those who know and love Mica appreciate her passion to celebrate birthdays—everyone's birthdays. She loves a joyous party and goes out of her way to remember the birthdays of the people God has placed in her life. "The day a person entered this world is worthy of a great celebration!" she says.

In July 2021, Mica joined me and fifteen other abortion survivors at our first-ever ASN retreat. Never before in history had this many survivors gathered together. Our event theme was "You Belong," and this same message was the next step in Mica's healing.

"All my life, I felt I didn't belong," she says. "After school, I didn't belong with those classmates who ran into the arms of their parents. I was an orphan. A foster child. Even when I was adopted, I didn't seem to belong among my cousins because so many of them looked and sounded like their parents and siblings and aunts and uncles and other cousins. I was different. I was adopted. But at that retreat, there were seventeen of us who, though our stories varied greatly, had one major thing in common. We were abortion survivors. We were chosen to live.

"For the very first time in my life," Mica says, "I looked around the room and felt that in this group, I truly belonged."

Micaella has made peace with the fact that much of her birth story will remain a mystery. Though her physical conditions demand ongoing care and limit some of her activities, she doesn't let them stop her from ministering to others. She is a gifted photographer and an ordained chaplain with a doctorate in Christian counseling. She speaks openly about her own story of survival and connects with others like her through ASN. Most important of all, she nurtures her relationship with God, her protector and heavenly Father, and she shares her faith with others.

Micaella's life exemplifies her message: *You are loved. You are chosen. You have a purpose.*

7

THE MYSTERIOUS BOND: JENNIFER'S STORY

Jennifer

JENNIFER GREW UP WONDERING ABOUT TWO MYSTERIES that date back as far as she can remember. The first mystery involved hearing her mother tell close friends and family that "Jennifer is my miracle baby." She wasn't quite sure what it meant when she was younger, but it made her feel special.

The second mystery involved an ongoing sense of missing someone. Jennifer says it's hard to describe the feeling; this is the best explanation she has: "It was as if I felt, even as a very young child, that I used to have someone with me all the time and that I no longer did. I sensed a gap. A hole. An aloneness that I couldn't explain or express."

Many years passed before Jennifer discovered what her mother meant by "miracle"—and that same discovery helped her finally solve the mystery of who was missing.

Jennifer didn't solve these mysteries all at once. There was no single turning point, no groundbreaking discussion with her mother. Instead, Jennifer gathered bits and pieces while growing up, often from conversations she overheard between her mother and others. Some details she discovered during her tween and teen years. Other details she uncovered through research as an adult. Jennifer is still uncertain about some of the specifics, and—since her mother passed away in 2012—she may never be able to confirm many of her conclusions.

Jennifer has shared what she knows of her story with me, and she has allowed me to now share that same story with you, my readers. I am honored that she trusted me with her history, because several parts of the account are still painful for her to discuss.

UNEXPECTED COMPLICATIONS

When Jennifer's mother (we'll call her Laura) was twenty-eight years old, she was the married mother of a two-year-old daughter. Evidently, Laura had a clandestine affair and became pregnant. Not wanting to expose the affair, she decided to have an abortion. Jennifer is not sure if the procedure took place at an abortion clinic or a hospital, but she does know that it occurred early in the pregnancy, probably at around eight weeks. The abortion seemed to go fine, and Laura returned home to her husband. Was her secret affair still secret? Jennifer doesn't know, but a couple of months later Laura started to feel a fluttering in her abdomen. Concerned, she went to her ob-gyn.

"You're pregnant," the doctor announced to a shocked Laura. Her doctor determined that Laura had been pregnant with twins. The abortion terminated the life of one twin, but the other had survived. As Laura reeled from this news, she learned that she still had time to abort the second child. Instead, she decided to carry the other twin—Jennifer—to term. To this day, Jennifer has no idea what Laura said to her husband about the pregnancy.

(Jennifer eventually tracked down the medical records from her birth and learned that complications with bleeding appeared during her mother's third trimester. The doctor suspected placenta previa—a condition where the baby's placenta is partially or totally covering the mother's cervix, thus blocking the birth canal. This condition can cause severe bleeding during pregnancy and delivery.[1])

Laura was admitted to a nearby hospital in Monterey, California, and given medication to delay her labor. Then she was transported to Stanford Hospital in Palo Alto, where an ultrasound showed no signs of placenta previa but revealed that the baby was in the breech position. The medical notes also indicated other potential risks, so the medical staff decided to perform an emergency C-section.

Jennifer was born July 18, 1980, nearly ten weeks early and weighing three pounds, one ounce. The medical records describe her as a "healthy, vigorous baby." Being so premature, however, Jennifer was placed in an incubator in the NICU at Stanford and was later transferred back to Monterey, where she remained hospitalized for two months. Despite the complications surrounding her birth, Jennifer did not experience any additional health concerns once she reached a healthy weight.

Fortunately for Jennifer, the medical staff kept notes about her mother's visits during her time in the hospital. These notes offer some insight into Laura's thought process before taking her infant daughter home.

"She was interested in caring for me," Jennifer says, "but apprehensive about bringing me home. She said she was planning on moving in a couple of weeks and would feel better then. One day she brought a baby book to the hospital and requested footprints. She told the nurses that she couldn't really afford the cost, but felt I was worth it."

Around this same time, Laura apparently told the nurses that she needed to straighten out a lot of family problems before bringing Jennifer home. Interestingly, the father listed on Jennifer's birth certificate is her older sister's father.

The day before Laura picked her up from the hospital, Jennifer says, her mother told the nurses that she was looking forward to Jennifer coming home.

The next few years are filled with unknowns. Jennifer does know that shortly after she was born, Laura got divorced.

"I know my mother had regrets about her divorce," Jennifer says, "because I remember her talking about how he was a good husband and provider, and she would have had a better life if she had stayed married to him. Obviously my birth changed that. I suspect she resented me for that."

It seemed to Jennifer that her mother favored her as a child. But the older she got, the angrier Laura became.

At some point during her childhood, Jennifer's birth father started coming around. She knows he was about ten years younger than her mother. Jennifer recalls him babysitting her and her older sister.

"I remember my father as being a fun, caring daddy," she says. "I loved spending time with him and have good memories. He was a good daddy to me, though he didn't live with us. I remember when he came to see me, I would run to his arms and he would pick me up. He taught me to tie my shoes and played with me."

Sadly, when Jennifer was about seven years old, her birth father was arrested and sent to prison. She never saw him again, though she learned that "he told the court to tell me he was sorry and he loved me." To this day, Jennifer has no idea of her father's whereabouts or whether he is still alive.

Laura remarried when Jennifer was seven years old. In 1991, when Jennifer was eleven, the couple had a son together. Unfortunately, this was around the time Jennifer says that her relationship with her mother began to deteriorate:

> It seemed to me that Mom became increasingly angry
> with me. She yelled a lot and was always upset about
> something. I remember feeling unloved, stressed, and
> anxious all the time. We tried to improve our situation
> by going to counseling, but unfortunately we never really
> got the chance to have a loving, close relationship. As I
> moved into my teen years, I couldn't stand living at home
> and would sneak out to friends' houses. I was rebelling
> against their authority. I couldn't focus on school, so
> I skipped sometimes. I'm sorry to say that I ended up
> choosing the wrong influences.

By the time Jennifer turned fifteen, she'd reached a turning point. Her mom and stepdad told her that she needed to leave their home, so she moved in with her boyfriend and his mother. Two years later, at seventeen, Jennifer married that same boyfriend. That's when their lives took a tragic turn. Her new husband resorted to crime as a way to put money in their pockets, and Jennifer retreated into depression and anxiety. Their relationship began to unravel.

By age eighteen, Jennifer was pregnant and feeling trapped. Unable to support a child, and in no condition to raise one, she chose what seemed like her only option—abortion. But that decision didn't make things better, and after four more years of marriage, the couple divorced and Jennifer began a long journey of healing.

FINDING FORGIVENESS

In the years that passed after those dark days, Jennifer came to a saving knowledge of Jesus Christ and gave her life to Him.

"God chose me. He saved me. He has given me life so I can share it with others," she says. She now has a tender heart for women who, like her mother and herself, have chosen abortion.

"I forgive my mother for the abortion," Jennifer says. "Having had an abortion myself years ago, I understand being in a place where you feel you have no other choice. It is a very difficult thing to go through, and the pain lasts for many years. I can't imagine what she was going through when she realized she was still pregnant with me—the shock and regret she must've felt. I wish we could've had a closer relationship and communicated more. We could've healed some of our wounds together. I do not have any negative feelings toward any of my family."

Jennifer has given much thought to her aborted twin. She's never lost that feeling of "missing" her aborted twin.

"What would it have been like," she wonders, "to have grown up with someone so close to me? For about the first two months of my life, I shared my mother's womb with a brother or sister. I am sad that I don't have my twin and miss him or her very much. I picture us as being so close and having a bond that is unbreakable. It is a grief that is unexplainable. It is truly amazing how God can create that kind of bond inside me with someone I have never met. As mysterious as it is, I do feel a strong spiritual connection."

A TESTIMONY TO HEALING

Jennifer recently participated in an ASN video project called Faces of Choice. In her segment, she says, "I believe that even though the situation could be viewed as tragic or sad, God has worked this out for good. . . . After having the Lord in my life, I've been able to appreciate more what I've been given. I have a beautiful life. I have children of my own, who are all sweet, intelligent, giving, and kind. I also have the greatest husband [Jimi], who is also my best friend. . . . I was not rejected. I was not forgotten. I am loved. I have a hope and I have a future. The same is true for you. No matter what you go through, you can choose to live free, joyous, and peaceful. You can choose to forgive others and have compassion."[2]

I've now known Jennifer for about ten years, and I've seen her kindness, her forgiveness, and her compassion up close and personal. She's a living testimony to the healing that God can bring to a heart surrendered to Him! I especially love her compassion for women who have experienced abortion. She understands what so many miss: Women who have had abortions, but then later experience grace and forgiveness, are also survivors. That truth may make some readers very uncomfortable.

As I explained in my own story, we are prone to see villains when we read a story. But Jesus sees hearts that are in need of grace, forgiveness, and love. It is my hope that Jennifer's story inspires that same kind of love in others, and in everyone who hears her story.

8

COLD WATER TO A THIRSTY SOUL: JULIAN'S STORY

Julian

JULIAN'S STORY BRINGS TO MIND THE WORDS OF PROVERBS 25:25: "Like cold water to a thirsty soul, so is good news from a far country." While at first glance his story seems like bad news upon bad news, when you view the events of Julian's life through an eternal lens, I trust you will see what Julian and I see—God refreshing thirsty souls amid earthly brokenness. And since Julian was born and currently resides in Sri Lanka, the good news of his story certainly comes from a faraway country.

I first became aware of Julian after he discovered ASN online. I couldn't help but notice how the culture of his country, which is very different from that of the United States, had shaped his life, and yet how much we have in common because of the lifelong effects of being abortion survivors.

Julian's characterization of his family's dynamics begins with a bit of cultural disconnect: "Before I was conceived," he says, "my mother was taken as a second bride by my father while he already had a legal spouse. He allowed his legal wife and their three children to continue to live at his home under his care and so chose bigamy. He seemed to be a loving parent to his children, but not a faithful husband to his first wife. He chose to have this new life amid the disapproval and condemnation of the people in his circle. My parents' actions resulted in shame and guilt and social stigma, leading the family into a great mess.

"Another issue beyond bigamy complicated my family's struggle with stigma—the tensions between two ethnic groups or races. My family belongs to a minority ethnicity in Sri Lanka, and the ethnic clashes on the island negatively affected my family and me. These tensions existed even before my parents were born, and were heightened by the contrast of Christian and Hindu beliefs and traditions. My father came from a traditional Christian family; my mother was from a Hindu family. When she married my father, she was parentless and had two younger brothers. She was thrown out of her family circle after her shameful decision; her brothers and relatives performed a funeral ritual. My father's decision to begin a romantic relationship with my mother, then marry her without divorcing his first wife, was viewed as shameful in both families and in Christian circles."

To make a complex situation even worse, after their marriage Julian's parents had two children of their own—a situation that introduced considerable tensions among the siblings. In addition to supporting his two wives and five children, Julian's father also took responsibility for the financial care of both his parents and his siblings. They all lived on a tea plantation near a small town situated in the Central Province of Sri Lanka, where Julian's father worked in a tea factory. His income was modest and the women did not work outside the home, so family finances were tight.

When the couple discovered they were expecting Julian, they did not take it as good news. Though neither parent ever told Julian exactly why they decided to abort him, he pieced together a number of possibilities based on family comments and circumstances: a large family that already had too many members; the financial stress of another child; an ongoing battle with the guilt, shame, and stigma stemming from his parents' bigamy and faith differences; plus the heightened tensions and resentment among the siblings.

So Julian's mother, with the support of her husband, consulted with some older women in their town who were experienced with Ayurvedic medicine—an ancient, holistic healing system first developed more than three thousand years ago in India. It is based on Hindu religious teachings and encompasses the belief that health and wellness depend on a delicate balance between the mind, body, and spirit. It combines natural treatments (mainly derived from plants and herbs, but that may also include animal products, metals, and minerals) with diet, exercise, and lifestyle adjustments.[1]

Julian's mother told him she took "medicines" that were meant to end the pregnancy. She later explained to Julian that these medicines made him "very sick." While Julian doesn't know exactly what his mother took, he certainly knows the consequences he suffered as a result, as he has paid the price for it his entire life. I'll let him explain it for himself.

"THROW AWAY THIS DOG"

I was born on July 13, 1980. My father was thirty-nine at the time and my mother thirty. According to my mother and my grandmother, I was a very feeble, bloody baby. I had blisters all over my body. I needed to be kept in the hospital after my mother was discharged, though I'm not sure how long I was there. My elder siblings urged my mother not to bring me home because of my weak and unpleasant condition. According to my mother, when one older sibling saw me, he yelled at her to "throw away this dog." Nevertheless, they had to tolerate my presence.

Beyond my weak body and blistered skin, the effects on my internal, mental, and emotional health were not known. To this day I don't know how many of the illnesses and challenges I suffered as a child—and still suffer as an adult—can be attributed to the substances my mother used in the abortion attempt. All my life I have suffered with chronic headaches, skin issues, multiple lipomas (small benign tumors that usually occur just beneath the surface of the skin), mitral valve regurgitation, bilateral inguinal hernia, and other conditions. I had to fight for my survival not only in my mother's womb, but in my father's home, too. My presence as part of the family seemed on the one hand to be unwelcome—not only as an infant, but as I grew into adolescence as well. On the other hand, I felt loved by my parents and to some extent my siblings. It was all very confusing. Life's challenges during my childhood suggested that maybe it would have been better if I'd been prevented from entering this broken world. I always felt bad about not belonging, not bonding with my brothers, being physically unfit and poor in sports. All this left me feeling moody, lonely, angry, unloved, and conflicted.

My Savior, however, provided direction that superseded any darkness or struggles I had. The Lord led me to personally accept Him as Savior and Lord when I was twelve years old. This relationship with the Lord, plus learning His Word, helped secure my identity. As a young adult, life seemed both a fiery furnace and as cold as ice. I had many ups and downs, but the good Lord always drew me closer to Him. His mysterious love is unfathomable. My childhood had its challenges, but the Lord enabled me to fight against the currents.

One event in particular stands out as an illustration of just how severe those currents were. It took place on the afternoon before my Advanced Level Examination (a test that takes place before students enter university) as I was studying for the exam at my home. I heard one of my male siblings quarreling with my stepsister. He had never liked me since my childhood and displayed great anger against me. I intervened to stop the fight, not knowing that I was placing myself in a life-threatening situation. My sibling brutally assaulted me, and he began to cut me with a pair of scissors. His intention seemed clear to those around me. He wanted to end my life.

I ran for help—I ran to save my life. He came hurtling after me. He broke through the ceiling above me and down into the room at my house where I was hiding. I squeezed myself through the iron bars outside the window and escaped from the room. He continued chasing me with the scissors. The drama continued until nightfall. I finally found refuge at the house of my uncle, who lived a few kilometers away. Someone brought my books and a school uniform late at night so I could go to my exam the following day. Only at the examination hall did I identify the wounds and bruises on my body. My classmates were shocked. They asked what had happened, but I maintained silence! The Lord helped me get through my examination amid the mess and trauma. I did not return to my home for a few months, since I was told that the threat level was still high.

My Creator and Sustainer, however, was still merciful and gracious. Without His help, I believe my life would have ended right then. But He had His hand on me. As was spoken by the prophet Isaiah, "A bruised reed he will not break, and a faintly burning wick he will not quench; he will faithfully bring forth justice" (Isaiah 42:3). I was bruised but not broken!

THE CALL TO MINISTRY

Beginning in adolescence, Julian became very interested in Christian ministry. He joined small groups and Bible studies and participated in evangelistic activities.

"Though the life of a full-time Christian worker and volunteer is not easy," he says, "I appreciate the fact that I was exposed to the mission field, the needs of people, service, and ministry. The Lord was hovering over me. He used people and circumstances to help encourage me. There are overseas missionaries who touched my heart. I thank God for the number of good people who touched my life."

With God's help, Julian maintained a positive relationship with his mother. In fact, both of Julian's parents made personal commitments to Jesus and became born-again believers. When Julian lost his father in 2004, his mother was essentially abandoned, at least as far as the family was concerned. Julian was the only one still caring for his mother. In 2009 he took her into his own home and cared for her until her death from cancer in 2014. Julian takes great comfort in knowing he was able to provide her with dignity and respect, medical care, palliative care, and a proper burial. It's a picture of redemption that the child whose mother chose abortion became the one to care for her in her years of need.

"When I was standing in my mother's graveyard as her coffin was being buried," Julian says, "I understood that the Lord protected *me* to look after *her*. I had to look after her after my father's death. She died from cancer, but she had great faith in God and never questioned God for her illness. She lived her last months on this earth as if she were never going to die."

A NEW CHAPTER OF HEALING

In spite of all the good God was doing in his life, Julian says, he still sensed a need for inner healing that seemed to elude him. I often hear these sentiments from other abortion survivors, but Julian had never met anyone who shared his experience and understood its impact. But then, in 2021, Julian reached out to ASN after discovering our organization online.

"ASN helped me rethink my life and reinterpret my struggles," he says. "I began to understand that most of the reasons for the problems in my life were due to the abortion attempt. ASN's resources provided me knowledge and understanding about who I really am, and helped me shape my perspective and approach toward the core issues of my life. They ministered to me, helping me forgive the past, let go of wrong beliefs, and work on the facts. Online meetings allowed me to hear from the facilitators, to draw insights, and also to learn from fellow survivors. ASN made me believe that I do have a family—a family of survivors. The Lord used ASN to empower me. I am confident that I can rise above the circumstances and challenges of my life. I thought it was only me who was broken, but my journey with ASN taught me that the world itself is broken and needs our help."

As I read Julian's correspondence with us at ASN, I was ecstatic! It was as if Julian was the poster child for all I'd prayed for—for everything I wanted ASN to be. It wasn't long before Julian volunteered to be an online group leader himself, and I am both impressed and grateful for how he contributes to the growth and well-being of others. He truly has a heart to help others through the experiences of his own life, bringing inspiration and edification to every encounter.

"I want my story to empower others," he says. "Let it be a reason for others to give thanks to God. My work with ASN helped me see that broken lives and broken families need to be cared for."

Julian is all about that kind of caring, and he's now had the added privilege of seeing God at work in the lives of some of his siblings. One of his siblings and one of his stepsiblings have even become pastors!

"I am still growing into maturity," he says. "I have learned that broken people have a place in this broken world. But when they are being transformed and start mending, they become effective tools to fix the world. I believe that the Lord still has enormous thoughts about me, as told in Psalm 139."

For you formed my inward parts;
   you knitted me together in my mother's womb.
I praise you, for I am fearfully and wonderfully made.
Wonderful are your works;
   my soul knows it very well.
My frame was not hidden from you,
when I was being made in secret,
   intricately woven in the depths of the earth.
Your eyes saw my unformed substance;
in your book were written, every one of them,
   the days that were formed for me,
   when as yet there was none of them.

PSALM 139:13-16

9

BEGINNINGS: AMY'S STORY

Amy with her husband and their children

CHILDREN WHO GROW UP WITH THEIR BIRTH PARENTS often delight in hearing stories about their beginnings. Amy, a mother of two, smiles at the memories of her children listening with rapt attention to the stories of their births. During Amy's childhood, on the other hand, she never heard such stories. Instead, Amy cherishes memories of turning again and again to a beloved children's book about being adopted.

Amy was never told the full story of her birth. Most of what she knows she pieced together based on some paperwork inside a file folder with her name on it. As she read through the file, she found several pages only partially filled out, containing just enough detail to spark questions, curiosity, and a desire to know more. Much more. Amy knows the outcome—her eventual adoption—but not all the events leading to that outcome. What little information she found felt like notes from an incomplete novel. But Amy's story is no novel. It is true—sadly and wonderfully true. And it is still being written.

On the surface, Amy's case file reads like many others: four pages of incomplete birth history from her birth mother, some information about the doctors, and a few details of the birth itself. When Amy went in search of her origin story as a young adult, that file left her with more questions than answers. *Who was my mother? What happened? Where was she a college student? In a nearby town? Why did she place me for adoption? Do I look like her? Does she ever think of me? How did this happen?*

Amy refers to the events of her physical birth as her "first beginning."

SO MANY QUESTIONS

The *knowns* of Amy's story:

- Amy's mother was a twenty-year-old college student. Her father, nineteen, was also a college student.
- The pregnancy was twenty-eight to thirty weeks along when Amy's mother first visited a physician on May 18, 1980.
- Amy was born just nineteen days later, on June 6, 1980, in Ashland, Oregon.

It is here, though, that the story takes a dramatic and astounding turn. Not only was the young mother's first doctor visit much later than usual—more than halfway through her pregnancy, and less than a month before Amy was born—the file shockingly indicates that this same visit is when this young woman first learned she was pregnant! Even more shocking is this line from her records:

"Apparently, mother went for a therapeutic abortion which was induced, and a viable infant was born."

In those few knowns, however, were still so many *unknowns*. How was this young woman pregnant for so long and unaware of it? Was she in denial? Did she immediately seek an abortion after accepting the reality of her pregnancy, or did she take some time to decide? What was life like for her in the days between her doctor visit and her abortion appointment? Did she wrestle with her decision? Did she share the decision with Amy's biological father, and did he support her? Did she tell her family? Her friends? Perhaps the support she expected from family or the father failed to materialize—or did she feel alone and decide that abortion was her only option?

Whatever the answers, at some point Amy's mother made the decision to end her unborn child's life just two and a half weeks after her first visit to the doctor.

Oregon's standards at the time required that the physician go before a medical board to justify why a third-trimester pregnancy should be terminated. Since there's no indication that this step ever took place, it is unclear if this young adult was aware of how far her pregnancy had advanced, if the doctor was also unaware, or if they both knew that the baby was definitely viable but proceeded with the abortion anyway. If they knew how far along she was, it would be imperative to initiate the procedure as soon as possible, requiring her to make a quick decision. For whatever reasons, Amy's mother apparently believed that the best way to deal with her unwanted pregnancy was to end it.

A SECOND BEGINNING

Meanwhile, Amy's *second* beginning was taking shape in a coastal Oregon town a few hours away. A young couple there, Richard and

Nancy, had hopes and dreams of starting a family of their own. Nancy often remarked that she wanted two girls, whom she would name Amy and Katie. As time passed with no babies, the couple's hurt and longing grew. It was a difficult period for both of them, especially since it seemed to Nancy that the other women around her were all having babies. After years of trying without success to have a child naturally, they turned to two big-city adoption agencies. And yet, for reasons that seemed both minor and confusing, both agencies turned them down. In the meantime, Nancy's brother successfully adopted two children.

Heartbroken and exhausted after seven years of waiting, watching, and wanting, Richard and Nancy finally gave up hope of having children of their own—biological or adopted. But one day, a neighbor who knew of their heartache ran to greet them as they exited their car. She was eager to share the name of an adoption agent in town who had "babies available." It was an interesting development, but the couple were hesitant to get their hopes up. Nancy in particular was afraid that they would be turned down yet again. Instead of the news sparking hope and excitement, Nancy cried out in grief: "I can't do this anymore!" She insisted that it was time to accept that their dream of becoming parents would never be fulfilled.

In the weeks that followed, God brought about a change in Nancy's heart. In the spring of 1980, the couple contacted the adoption agency that their neighbor had felt so driven to tell them about. Now all they could do was wait.

On June 5, 1980, in a clinic several hours away in Ashland, Oregon, a third-trimester abortion procedure began. The particular method used that day was not specified; the records note only that Amy's mother was "induced for an abortion." The records are also spotty and incomplete. The file notes state that the baby was in a "normal, head-down presentation" and that "bag and mask oxygen were required at delivery." At 12:35 a.m. on June 6, 1980, Amy made her unexpected live appearance. She survived what millions of other babies have not.

"As a result of a started abortion procedure," Amy says, "I was born—alive."

The fact that she arrived in the middle of the night raises additional questions. Why wasn't the abortion completed during typical office hours? What happened to change the situation from a planned abortion to the delivery of a live infant? Did Amy's mother change her mind mid-procedure? Did the physician freak out when he realized just how far along the baby was? Unfortunately, no more information is available. Amy can only wish that she knew more of this woman's story.

The little girl who arrived in the early hours of the morning was a tiny thing, weighing in at three pounds, six ounces, with a bit of reddish hair. Given no name, the infant was immediately transported from Ashland to nearby Medford, Oregon, where she was hospitalized for several weeks in the NICU. The nuns at the hospital doted on the anonymous child and prayed for her. The hospital staff noted in her records that this little one was determined to survive.

Within weeks of Richard and Nancy's visit to the local adoption agency, Amy's birth mother decided to pursue an adoption placement with the same agency.

During a staff meeting where available babies were presented—with details about where they were located, their current situations, and so on—an adoption agent named Marian learned about this particular preemie. She immediately thought of a young couple who had recently come to see her. The wife was a nurse and would know how to care for a fragile infant.

Marian quickly spoke up: "That one is mine!"

It wasn't long before Marian called the young couple to tell them about a tiny girl who had entered the world early after surviving an abortion attempt. The baby was nearing NICU graduation in a large hospital in Medford. Were they interested?

In early July, Richard and Nancy drove to the hospital to meet this little fighter. True to their personalities, Richard was calm and steady while Nancy was nervous and frightened. Both were overjoyed at the thought of bringing this precious newborn home.

However, agency rules would not let them take the baby home right away. The couple would be required to meet the baby in the hospital and spend the night in a nearby hotel to sleep on the decision. The following day, if they still wanted the baby, they could take her home. Oh, how impatient these prospective parents were! They did not want to wait one extra moment for their new family life to begin. They knew this was their girl before they even met her.

Yet they were surprised during the hospital visit when they noticed an unusual mark on the top of the baby's head. Was it an injury sustained during birth? No one had told them about that. What was it, exactly, and what did it mean for the girl's future? The doctor on duty at the time only said to go home and "watch it" as she grew. "Watch for *what*?" Nancy asked, though she never received a satisfying answer. The adoption medical report referred to it as a "birthmark on fontanelle." (The bright-red birthmark didn't go away until she was two to three years old.)

The following morning, Richard and Nancy went to pick up their girl from the hospital. It seemed like the baby was heaven sent, as she was surrounded by nurses—nuns dressed all in white—lovingly tending to her. Nancy later told her daughter, "They carried you out and helped me put you in the car and prayed over you."

The adoption was made official on February 9, 1981. About two years later, Nancy became pregnant and brought home a little sister for Amy named Katie.

WHEN NOTHING COMES EASY

Nancy was, and still is, quite a go-getter. She knew something wasn't right about her infant's development and visited numerous doctors and specialists, who began to monitor Amy. Nancy was always pressing them, asking, "What does my daughter have?" She and Richard presumed that because of the attempted abortion, Amy had sustained an injury to her brain. But they didn't know what that injury was, or how it would affect their precious daughter's future.

When Amy was about two years old, a pediatric orthopedist diagnosed her with cerebral palsy. The doctor explained that two leading causes of cerebral palsy are brain injury and oxygen deprivation during birth, and that cerebral palsy can manifest in a variety of ways. For Amy, her cerebral palsy means that she wears hearing aids and experiences weakness, muscle tightness, and balance issues with her legs.

During Amy's early years, doctors often made various negative, distressing, and pessimistic comments about her prognosis. Some specialists told Richard and Nancy that Amy might never walk, or that she might have to be institutionalized. Then her parents found a doctor in Seattle with a much more positive outlook—one who encouraged them to have the same.

"Enjoy her successes, show her stuff, give her experiences, dwell on positives, not negatives," he said. His positive outlook lifted the burden from Nancy and Richard and helped them see beyond the dire scenarios the other physicians predicted. It turns out that

Amy continued to grow and thrive, exceeding the expectations of those previous doctors.

Though Amy was too young to understand most of what was being said about her, the same preemie who fought so hard to live in the NICU now fought hard to walk, run, skip, ride her bike, and learn just like her peers. She also learned to compensate for some of her limitations.

"I couldn't walk, but I could climb," Amy recalls. "I would scoot and walk on my knees to get where I was going. I loved swimming. It was one of the only things that ever made me feel weightless and free." Even in the water, it was hard for Amy to kick her legs smoothly, and outside the water she had to wear leg braces and special shoes.

Riding a bike was especially difficult. Amy found it tough to coordinate arms and legs that wouldn't cooperate. She was probably ten years old before she could ride a bike without falling. In fourth and fifth grade she played basketball on the "B" team. When running sprints at practice, she was typically the last to finish.

Schoolwork did not come easily either. "I wasn't different enough to require special education," Amy says, "but man, did I struggle! I couldn't focus on my work. I couldn't make sense of math equations and basic math facts." It was clear that some of her teachers didn't know what to do with her. As a result, some didn't seem to even try. It was also distressing for Amy when teachers compared her with her accomplished younger sister.

Amy struggled not only academically but socially as well. Making friends was a challenge, and even when she did have success, she was impulsive and often did things that struck other children as weird or awkward.

One day when Amy was in fourth grade, a special education teacher singled her out during recess in front of some other girls whom Amy really wanted to be her friends. He crouched down to her eye level, waved very obviously, and said—loudly and slowly—"Hi, Amy. I know you." The rest of what he said was lost to her. She simply stood there, feeling mortified.

Amy unfortunately let that experience shape her self-esteem and her identity as a "weak, disabled kid." Looking back, she doesn't think the teacher meant to embarrass her. He'd probably heard that she was hard of hearing and simply wanted to connect with her. Whatever the teacher's intent, the incident caused Amy to be bitter toward him for years and years.

Also during fourth grade, probably in part because of this same teacher, Amy started hating herself. "I didn't think I measured up," she says. "I didn't have anyone I considered 'my people,' and I was angry with God, feeling like He had messed up on me."

It required intensive work on Amy's part to achieve the age-appropriate physicality that seemed to come easily and naturally to her peers. Amy fought for every advancement and achievement she made, which meant weekly physical therapy appointments and longer drives at least twice a month to visit specialists. It was all quite exhausting, both for Amy and her parents.

School, meanwhile, never got any easier—but with hard work and dedication, Amy was able to achieve her goals.

At first, inspired by her own childhood experiences, Amy considered a career in physical therapy. She was comfortable around PTs, and after high school she worked in a clinic as a PT aide. Amy even job shadowed some PTs, but her plans changed when she learned about occupational therapy and met some kids who received OT.

"The kids were *amazing*!" Amy says. "I felt like that was a better fit for me." She shifted direction and is now blessed to work as a child occupational therapist. OT is an ideal fit for her, a line of work she loves. It's a career through which she is able to give back what she received from her own therapists, helping the next generation of children overcome obstacles and reach goals of their own.

Amy enjoys her career so much that it sometimes doesn't even feel like work, but more like building relationships with children and helping them work through the challenges they face. She is continually humbled by the children she helps—children who often teach her and bless her with their own stories. Thanks to her own background, she feels like she is able to understand these kids at a deeper level than some other therapists.

As a young adult, forming romantic relationships was just as difficult for Amy as making friends. When a young man would ask Amy out, she struggled with how to tell him that she wore hearing aids and had cerebral palsy. But when she met Jason, for some reason it was easier. They got married in 2004 and now have two children. "Jason is my rock in this world," Amy says.

FINDING ANSWERS

Amy's parents never hid the fact that she had been adopted. They even gave her a book about being adopted—the one she turned to time and again when she was younger. She had, on occasion, tried to ask questions about her birth mother. Her parents' response was always the same—they became emotional yet remained quiet. She attributed their reluctance to her size and vulnerability at birth, her ongoing health issues, and her adoptive parents' hard work to provide the care she needed.

Her desire for answers only grew when Amy had her son, Eli, in 2010, and again in 2012, when she had her daughter, Emily. In October 2016, Amy was at work when a woman she admired mentioned making an adoption plan for her baby. On her way home that same day, Amy stopped by her parents' house to ask them about finding her birth mother. She wanted to thank the woman for giving her life. To Amy's surprise, her father blanched, spun, and walked out of the room. Her mom didn't know what to say.

"Um, um, uh . . ." she stammered. Then, in a hopeful tone, she asked, "Are you sure you don't want to journal your thoughts?"

Amy was confused. "No. Why would I want to journal?"

Amy's mother twice tried to respond, but twice stumbled over her words. Finally, she said abruptly, "I'd like to check in with Marian"—Amy's adoption agent.

When Amy left that night, she thought, *That was awkward.* Clearly something was up. Her parents' response was beyond the usual edginess she'd experienced when asking questions before. This time was different—very different.

Early the next morning, Amy opened her front door to find her mother standing there with two Starbucks cups in hand. Amy knew something was up—first, because her mother was very aware that Amy is not a morning person, but also because she seemed reluctant to enter the house. She handed Amy one of the cups but didn't look her in the eye. "I want you to hear the truth from me rather than finding out on your own."

"Mom, just tell me," Amy said. "What is it?"

"The truth is, Amy, your birth mom didn't go to the doctor because she was in early labor with you. She went to get an abortion . . . and you survived."

Time stood still. Shock zipped through Amy; the news rocked her to her core. She never imagined there was any history other than what she'd been told growing up.

Amy had questions, of course, but her mother wouldn't stay. Confused by that, Amy closed the door quietly behind her. As unsettled as she felt, things started to make sense as the day went on. She kept realizing, *Oh, that's why . . .*

Amy's mother had clearly hoped this information would never come out. And even though the secret was now exposed, another few years passed before Amy's mother opened the safety deposit box that contained Amy's original birth certificate, her medical notes, and a few pages of an interview with her birth mother. Amy immediately noticed that the first page of the interview was missing. Her mother apologized and said she felt bad for tearing up that page, admitting to Amy that the information had bothered her tremendously. Amy suspects that her mother—a strong-willed momma bear who is fiercely protective of her children—has always wished she could erase that part of Amy's history.

"If I'm being honest," Amy says, "at first I was ticked at my parents for keeping my story under such tight wraps and destroying information that was part of *my* story." But Amy says she could never tell Richard and Nancy about those feelings because she understands that her parents were only doing what they felt was best for their child.

Amy trusts that God, in His mercy, appointed two special people in need of a child to be the protectors of a little girl who had survived an awful thing.

When Amy told her husband what her mother had told her, Jason was just as surprised by what had been hidden all those years. In general, Amy's parents had always seemed so honest and open. But once he heard the truth, Jason also found that certain things now made more sense. Right away, he encouraged Amy to learn as much as she could about her birth and birth mother. But both of them wisely realized that Amy wasn't quite ready to pursue more answers. She needed time—time to process things the way *she* needed to.

The couple learned that Amy wasn't the only one who had made such a discovery. "You know there are other survivors," Jason quietly mentioned. A few times he encouraged Amy to watch videos of abortion survivors like Gianna Jessen and me, but Amy had no interest. Jason gently persisted, telling Amy about some of Gianna's physical issues and how he thought there were some strong similarities between her and Amy since they both dealt with spastic cerebral palsy. This information piqued Amy's interest, and she secretly watched the clips. But she was still reluctant to share her story.

REVISITING THE PAST

Amy's life—especially in recent years—has been a journey punctuated with burning questions and a great yearning to know who she is, where she came from, and about the woman who unintentionally gave her life. But she didn't know if she could—or should—try to learn more.

Eventually Amy started digging for more information. She has spoken with lawyers, doctors, adoption agency workers, hospital staff, the Oregon Health Authority, and anyone else she could think of. As she continues to search, she prays for patience and strength in how she responds to both people and information. Frankly, she says, it has been hard to deal with revisiting such a difficult past.

"I don't know if I'll ever fully understand why I survived when others didn't get that opportunity," she says. Yet searching for answers and processing the information she discovers has helped her learn to better accept herself. "Now, instead of feeling like a disabled person who doesn't measure up to others, I think *survivor*."

Amy says the journey has also allowed her to love more deeply than she ever thought possible. "When this started," she says, "the idea of loving someone who chooses an abortion was honestly hard for me. But then God placed strategic people in my life who've had an abortion. Through their stories, I have a better understanding of them and have developed compassion for them. Now I believe that we all need to link arms and share our stories—post-abortive women and survivors alike!"

No longer hiding her story, Amy hopes and prays that telling it can help others, including the biological parents who began her story—and almost ended it. God has given her a heart of compassion for her birth mother that she never thought was possible. For many years she hoped to one day connect with her birth mother, to let her know that she has a heavenly Father who loves her very much.

July 2021 was a turning point for Amy. She was finally able to track down her birth mother's location and write her a letter—just enough to let her birth mother know that she is alive, that she is well, and that she has a wonderful family and job. To her great joy and surprise, her birth mother wrote back, telling Amy she thinks about her every year around her birthday. It's another small beginning, and Amy hopes more communication will follow.

Amy's original identity emerged from her disability. Her struggle with cerebral palsy made her feel *different*—even more different than being adopted made her feel. And it's an identity she will always carry.

"[My disability is] a *part* of who I am," she says. "However, it's not *who* I am. There's a difference there, one that I hope the world sees. I have mild cerebral palsy and hearing loss, but I am so much more than that. I am a person—an individual with my own thoughts and feelings. I am Amy."

Moreover, her true identity is not in her disability, in her adoption, or in her having survived an abortion. "My identity," she says, "is in Christ."

Amy prays that her ultimate story will be one of love, forgiveness, and inspiration for anyone who hears it. From little beginnings came big blessings.

"I am not just a 'clump of cells,'" Amy says. "No one is. I fully believe that every child is a prized creation, and that God loves and protects His creation. His most prized creation is human life. One thing I love imagining when thinking about my beginnings is my heavenly Father saying *Not this one. This one is mine.*"

10

THE STRENGTH OF HOPE: HOPE'S STORY

Hope

TONYA WASN'T SURE WHAT SHE WAS "SUPPOSED" TO FEEL as she left the abortion clinic that spring day in 1991, but she didn't expect the burden of regret she now carried. It hung over her in the recovery room. It nagged at her as she gingerly climbed into the passenger seat for the drive back from the clinic. It intensified when she returned home to her two children.

But regret wasn't the only thing Tonya carried. Though she had no idea at the time, she was still carrying the baby she thought she'd just aborted.

The ten-and-a-half-week-old girl inside her had survived the D&C procedure, but not without damage. She had been struck and seriously injured by the steel loop of the curettage instrument. Still tucked away inside Tonya's womb, the baby was fighting for her life. The wondrous news is that she was a fighter—and still is more than thirty years later!

Tonya tried to resume her normal life, but nothing seemed normal at all. She was twenty-two years old and raising her two children alone while going through a divorce. As the weeks passed and she watched her two children, Tonya couldn't help but reflect on the baby she'd aborted. She found herself keeping track of how far along in the pregnancy she would have been, and the baby's corresponding stages of development. Weeks turned to months, but Tonya's regret remained.

Her busy life made it possible to keep pushing those negative thoughts back to the far reaches of her mind. That is, until the day she felt a fluttering in her abdomen. Almost any woman who's been pregnant recognizes that all-too-familiar feeling—the movement of life within her. A flood of emotions swept over Tonya. Shock. Fear. Then a powerful surge of hope. *Could it really be?* Tonya made an appointment with her doctor and discovered that she was five and a half months pregnant.

How did this happen? What should I do now? Is the baby okay? Questions and concerns looped through her mind. The same circumstances that first led her to the abortion clinic were still present in her life. She had made a host of poor choices leading up to this pregnancy. *Could I provide for another child? Do I have the capacity to parent three kids alone?*

Yet she couldn't deny another feeling stirring within her: love. Months of regret over the abortion were replaced with a desire to protect and provide for the tiny life within her. Driven by love, Tonya finally settled on a plan. She would find a private adoption attorney and place the baby in the arms of a loving family. She ached at the thought of giving up her third child, yet she knew it was in the child's best interests. She had a few months left before her October due date—enough time to find the ideal family.

But on August 12, 1991, that timeline changed drastically. Tonya went into premature labor and delivered a three-pound, six-ounce baby girl. Yet the miracle of the baby's survival was quickly overshadowed by the horrible reality of exactly what she had survived. The skin and skull from her forehead to her right ear had been cut away, leaving her brain partially exposed. Her medical records state that "the jagged edges of the skull and open scalp have the appearance of an old wound."

The D&C abortion attempt had clearly injured her. The baby was immediately rushed to the NICU, where she was placed on a breathing machine. Brain bleeds, brain damage, and a diagnosis of cerebral palsy meant the infant's survival was improbable at best. Tonya vividly recalls how her tiny daughter needed to be resuscitated four times that first night in the hospital, but—fighter that she was—she came back every time.

Over the next three months in the hospital, Tonya's baby defied the odds. Though the extent of her disabilities was still unclear, she was a child who made the improbable possible. What was no longer possible, though, was the simple adoptive placement that Tonya had hoped for when she learned that the abortion had failed. The child's special needs had been unexpected; now her future was uncertain.

Will I find someone who'll want her and be able to love her and provide for all her needs? The question plagued Tonya, even as she visited the hospital every day. Whether talking to her baby, singing to her, or praying for her, Tonya's time with her child was full of love. Yet in the midst of that joy there was pain, as additional special needs continued to appear.

Dear Lord, Tonya prayed, *let me be strong enough to give her the family she needs.* She also prayed for her child's future: *Lord, help me find a family who can love her as much as I do.*

A mother's love can't be aborted. Just as her child continued to grow, so did Tonya's love for her. That same love, once intermingled with uncertainty, now blossomed. This child was no longer an unwanted pregnancy; she was Tonya's flesh and blood, fighting to survive. In Tonya's view, she'd been given a second chance to do what was right. The abortion had seemed right for *her,* but this time she was determined to do right for her *child.* Coming face-to-face with her baby's humanity brought out Tonya's maternal instinct.

Once her child's odds of survival had improved, Tonya approached a Christian adoption agency to make an adoption plan. Despite the impending sense of loss that Tonya felt, she now understood adoption as putting her child's best interests ahead of her own desires. After she signed the adoption paperwork, it wasn't long before Tonya received a call from the agency. Terri Hoffman and her husband, Blair, were interested in adoption.

A NEW FAMILY IS BORN

As Terri heard the description of the baby's surprising, almost miraculous, circumstances, she realized that almost nothing about this girl's story fit the plans she and Blair had in mind for adoption—except one thing: They'd often discussed adopting a child with special needs. During her high school years, Terri had volunteered in a special education classroom and with the Special Olympics. She'd even considered a degree in special education before she decided to pursue nursing.

Terri and Blair's original vision involved adopting a little boy—maybe two to three years old and probably with special needs. But a tiny baby girl with an unknown future and undefined medical needs? *This isn't what we planned,* Terri thought, *but could it be what God has planned for us?* She wasn't sure, yet she couldn't shake the feeling that this was *their* daughter she was learning about. They didn't make a hasty decision. They spent time in prayer and interacting with other families who had experience with caring for children with special needs.

"What is the baby's name?" Terri asked the adoption agency.

"I'm sorry, but due to confidentiality rules we can't tell you the child's name at this point," the agent said. But Terri found herself scribbling a name on a piece of paper: "Hope." It seemed to leap directly from her heart to her pen.

Merriam-Webster defines *hope* as "desire accompanied by expectation." The word felt like a perfect fit. The couple decided that this little girl must be the child for whom they had prayed, so they moved forward with the adoption.

Hope's name came easily to Terri and Blair, but meeting her face-to-face was much more difficult. First, there were adoption agency rules to follow. Second, the hospital staff had grown very protective of the child, just as they'd grown protective of Tonya thanks to her daily visits. Two photographs of Hope were as much as the Hoffmans would see of their daughter-to-be until the day she went home with them.

The hospital staff wanted Hope to weigh at least six pounds before she was discharged. The adoption agency trained a foster mom to care for Hope when she was first discharged from the hospital, and this same foster mother would then instruct Terri and Blair once the adoption was final.

Hope was deeply loved—first by God, then by Tonya, the hospital team, and even the foster mother, who visited the girl numerous times and reported to the Hoffmans regarding the wonderful care Hope was receiving.

"You know, I, too, am falling in love with this baby. If you don't adopt her, I will," the foster mom told Terri one day. "And I'm so pleased to let you know that Hope is nearly always being held by someone—the nurses and volunteers. The nurses have even decorated her crib."[1]

A little over a month after Hope was born, Terri made the following journal entry:

SEPTEMBER 17, 1991

> Lord, I pray for this little girl and know Your hand is upon her. Pour out Your love on her when she is alone with no one to hold her. Bring her joy, Lord. Bless her, Lord, and heal her body. Keep Your hand upon her and a sparkle in her eye so that those who see her will know she is a miracle child. No matter what the circumstance or suffering, give her HOPE because Your hand is upon her.[2]

Terri's prayers joined Tonya's, uniting the hearts of two mothers before they ever met.

While the foster mom was preparing to care for Hope, the Hoffmans realized they also needed to get ready. They watched videos on how to care for an infant, their church threw them baby showers, and they readied their home. Their faith gave them increased strength, and that strength gave them increased faith.

Terri researched Hope's medical conditions, trying to understand what the future might hold. But when she consulted with a doctor about Hope's potential prognosis, Terri received an unexpected reply.

"Find another child," the doctor advised. "There are a lot of children out there. She's too sick. Find a healthy one."[3] A registered nurse herself, Terri knew that a prognosis is not a destination but a road map. She was more determined than ever to help Hope thrive.

On November 17, 1991, at three months of age and tipping the scales at six pounds, six ounces, Hope met her new parents for the first time. At first Terri stood by, taking in the beauty of the moment while waiting for an invitation from the adoption agency staff to approach. Even from a distance, she could see that Hope was alert and content. Blair, meanwhile, stepped forward and lifted her without hesitating. The couple's arms weren't empty from that day forward.

Does a mother ever forget the day she first laid eyes on her child? Hope was a beautiful baby, with a white-and-pink floral headband perfectly placed to cover the puckered skin on her forehead. The "kissing spot," as Terri called it, was formed by the cranial surgery completed to close up Hope's scalp. That outward sign, that scar, is a painful reminder of the attempted abortion. Yet it is also a testament to the power of love—of more than thirty years' worth of kisses planted firmly on that spot.

Hope's headband wasn't all she came home with that day. From the nurses she had a Minnie Mouse doll that squeaked to get her attention, and from Tonya she had a stuffed giraffe that played lullabies to bring her comfort—two reminders of how much Hope was loved from her very first days.

Terri remembers vividly how baby Hope would lay her right palm open on her scar, as if she was protecting it or maybe remembering something. Almost daily there were new revelations about just how much damage the abortion attempt had wrought and what it might mean for Hope's future.

Hope was six months old when Terri noticed the infant was still manifesting the startle reflex—well past the point when such a response should disappear completely. Terri once counted twenty-five such events in just one day. Related epileptic seizures, fairly common among children with cerebral palsy as a result of brain damage, were added to Hope's list of complications. Terri and Blair were happy to have more answers about Hope's condition, but they were also grieved by yet more obstacles.

As an infant, Hope didn't respond well to touch; her body remained stiff as a result of the cerebral palsy. Terri tried to imagine what the future held for Hope when, as an infant, everyday actions like talking or even laughing stiffened her body. But ask anyone who knows Hope today, and they'll tell you that she gives the best hugs. That ability didn't come quickly or easily, but it did come eventually. Hope first hugged Terri at fourteen months of age after playing in a pool. Turns out she was so relaxed from the water that she could stretch her arms around her mother.

Throughout her childhood, Hope continued to experience convulsive seizures. Moreover, she has endured multiple medical procedures since birth, from the scalp closure to tendon-release and back surgeries. Enduring all this alongside Hope hasn't been easy for Terri and Blair. It's frightening to face the fragility of life, yet Terri notes, "God is in control and we have to focus on today. None are guaranteed tomorrow. When you have a sick child, tomorrow doesn't matter, today does."

Remembering how God spared Hope's life in the womb has comforted Terri, Blair, and Tonya in times when Hope faced medical crises. If He saved her then, they figured, then He could save her again. And He has.

MOVING FORWARD

Hope has received nearly constant care since birth. The injuries stemming from the failed abortion may have slowed her down, but they've never stopped her. Her body doesn't always do what she wants it to do, but her determination is strong! With the love and support of so many, Hope has enjoyed a life filled with scouting activities, middle school dances, zip-lining, boating, wheelchair soccer, and even swimming with dolphins. Hope has experienced profound happiness and exudes great joy.

Despite the obstacles she faced, Hope never gave up on earning her high school diploma. She graduated in 2010, receiving a hard-earned standing ovation from the crowd of three thousand.

Hope is now in her early thirties. She likes to connect with audiences and has spoken at numerous events with Terri over the years. In particular, she routinely shares her story at high schools during disability awareness events. Like many young women her age, Hope also dreams of getting married someday, but she doesn't worry about the future. "If my plan doesn't work out," she says, "God's plan will be better."

God's plan for Hope and her relationship with her birth mother, Tonya, took a major leap forward in the later years of her childhood. Since Hope's infancy, the Hoffmans exchanged photos and letters with Tonya through the adoption agency. They typically sent a yearly update and usually heard from Tonya each year around Hope's birthday. Terri continued to pray for Tonya, in particular praying that someday they could all meet to show their love for Hope in person.

In her heart, it was as if Hope had always known Tonya. The

Hoffmans told Hope about the circumstances of her birth and adoption at an early age, and Hope had never demonstrated anger toward her birth mother, just gratitude and love.

When she was eleven years old, Hope asked about her birth mother more specifically. Her class had read a book about adoption, and suddenly she had so many questions. That very day, the Hoffmans got a letter from Tonya, a letter in which Tonya remarked, "Please let me know if anything ever happens to our girl."

The letter prompted Terri to wonder, *Is it time?*

Another year passed before Terri decided that the time had finally come.

"I always thought I would be ready when this day came, but when it happened, I was unprepared," Tonya said. She was deeply afraid that Hope might be mad at her, but she also knew it was time to make peace with herself and with God, and to welcome Hope into her life.

Emotions ran high as they all made plans to finally meet. There was excitement at first, followed by feelings of apprehension as the day of the meeting neared. And why not? This reunion, after all, was twelve years in the making.

"I missed you." These were Hope's first words once she steered her wheelchair up to greet Tonya. "Do you remember me from being in your belly?" Hope asked.

"I've remembered you every day," Tonya replied.

The day was joyous. They all went shopping and had lunch together. Terri, although along for the visit, watched it all as more of an onlooker. This was Hope and Tonya's time together, not hers. She didn't feel threatened; only blessed to witness their reunion. Hope, meanwhile, was excited and talkative.

Photos from that first meeting reveal what a strong physical resemblance Hope bears to Tonya. Honey-brown hair and infectious smiles. Faces that reflected the love and joy both had for one another. Yet feelings of guilt and regret also nagged at Tonya that day. She had surely done something right in placing Hope for adoption, but seeing her in that wheelchair . . .

Tonya continues to heal from the painful decisions she made regarding Hope's life, and they've since shared their stories together at Hope's church—an opportunity that blessed everyone present with incredible inspiration. Tonya sees the hand of God directing both Hope's life and her own. "She's here to teach us about life and true faith," Tonya says.

Hope has been doing exactly that—teaching others about life and faith—since before she was born. As Hope has shared publicly: "Being small, different, or not yet born doesn't change who we are. I am much more than a choice."

She's *Hope*, and she's a miraculous reminder of both the beauty and the value of every life.

11

A TRANSFORMED HEART: JOSIAH'S STORY

Josiah

THIRTEEN-YEAR-OLD JOSIAH SAT FROZEN in place as he tried to wrap his head around his parents' words.

He was an abortion survivor?

Wait. What?

This new information seemed at odds with the adoption story he'd known all his life. Since he was very young, Josiah's parents had described adoption as a beautiful gift. He understood that birth parents sometimes couldn't care for their child for some important reason, yet they loved that child so much that they arranged for him or her to be raised by a loving adoptive family. That had been Josiah's story, just as it was the story for ten of his twelve siblings. His two eldest brothers were the only ones with a different story, the only siblings who weren't adopted.

Josiah has always appreciated the fact that his family is vibrantly pro-life and that adoption was their way of living out their beliefs. His dad was the worship pastor at their church and advocated being pro-life as a way of living out the gospel. In fact, the family's first decision to adopt took place at a Christian crisis pregnancy center where his mother volunteered. Josiah's mother counseled a pregnant woman to choose life rather than abortion, and the woman in turn asked her to adopt her child—so she did! His parents had lots of love to give, and since then the family has grown, one adoption at a time.

Like his older sister, Josiah was adopted from South Korea. His adoptive parents learned of Josiah in an adoption agency's news-letter. He was described as a child with special needs because one of his arms was deformed. Josiah spent the first thirteen months of life in a foster home in South Korea. When his prospective parents saw the newsletter description, they felt drawn to Josiah and were thrilled that he was still available for adoption.

TEENAGE STRUGGLES

At age thirteen, Josiah listened as his parents said he was mature enough to know the rest of his story. It felt good to hear that his parents thought of him as mature. He wanted to live up to their confidence, so he listened intently as they described everything they knew. Two months into her pregnancy, Josiah's birth mother had undergone a D&C abortion. (This was most likely the cause of Josiah's deformed right arm.) Three months later, at five months along, she discovered she was still pregnant. Since the abortion had clearly failed, she decided to place her baby for adoption when he was born in 1995.

Josiah's image of a loving birth mother who wanted the best

for her child was gone in a flash. She had tried to abort him! And, when that didn't work, she gave him away. Anger surged in Josiah's heart, but he didn't show it. He held it in. In the weeks and months that followed, Josiah's anger took root and began to fester, prompting hatred toward his birth parents. Abortion was killing, so how could they choose to kill their own child?

It didn't help that at thirteen, Josiah was already struggling with his self-image. He had always been self-conscious about his arm, but that arm now became the symbol of his parents' attempt to end his life. Was he so worthless that the two people who should have loved him most actually wanted him dead?

The hurt ran deep. Josiah felt broken. Depression set in. Still, he kept his feelings to himself. They only surfaced when other frustrations brought him to a boiling point, and that's when he'd explode. His parents, however, never caught on. After all, he was a teenager—volatile emotions and outbursts just came with the territory, right?

Some teens struggling with anger turn away from God and the church. Josiah did the opposite—he immersed himself in being the "good Christian kid," but for all the wrong reasons. Josiah liked the way it made him look, and for the next few years he built his image on playing the part. He liked having other parents point to him as a role model. He relished being the "answer man" in youth group discussions. Desperate to compensate for the disturbing feelings of anger and hatred, Josiah strove to look good on the outside while on the inside he was steaming. He'd always felt that abortion was wrong, but now he demonized pro-abortion activists and women who'd had abortions. He built his identity on being the model Christian kid, albeit one with hatred in his heart. He felt the disconnect but never tried to address it. For three years Josiah was haunted by depression and hidden anger.

At age sixteen Josiah attended a summer church camp. There he came face-to-face with the truth. The Lord convicted him of his pride, arrogance, and pretense. Josiah realized that his identity and worth were not in what he did to earn the admiration and respect of others, but in what Jesus Christ had already done on the cross *for* him. Thoroughly convicted, Josiah surrendered his broken, hateful heart to God.

Josiah emerged from camp on a new path. He was ready to live a life of purpose and security. He knew he needed to forgive his birth parents, and—in return—*he* needed to be forgiven for the hatred he'd harbored against them. And not only them, but against anyone who'd ever participated in or supported abortion. Jesus died so that Josiah's sins might be forgiven, so how could he harbor resentment and unforgiveness against others? He felt God soften his heart and change his attitude. He knew God was transforming him from the inside out.

As Josiah heard more pro-life speakers, he found himself deeply moved by story after story from women who described being coerced to have abortions, or threatened that they would lose everything and everyone if they didn't choose abortion. He understood for the first time how wrong he had been to demonize such people. The words Jesus spoke as He was being nailed to the cross now echoed in Josiah's own spirit: "Father, forgive them, for they know not what they do" (Luke 23:34). He could see how many people were simply blinded, believing that abortion was the right answer, the best answer, or their only answer. For the first time, Josiah truly grasped the price so many paid for having an abortion—the pain, the regret, the guilt, and the emptiness that so many suffered for years, and that many still suffer today. In addition to forgiveness, something else grew inside Josiah: compassion.

At seventeen, Josiah spoke to his parents about helping him

contact the adoption agency that had worked with his birth parents. He wanted to know more of their story. The adoption agency sent Josiah what information they had. At the time of his conception, his birth parents were unmarried but living together. They already had one daughter when they learned of the pregnancy, and because of financial difficulties, they decided to seek an abortion about two months into the pregnancy. This information helped give Josiah a tender heart toward his birth parents. He could see how God had used the situation to bring Josiah to the United States, where he was welcomed by a good, loving, and godly family. God hadn't abandoned Josiah, but had rather spared his life and put into action a different, beautiful plan.

Motivated anew, Josiah began sharing his story. Throughout high school, college, and beyond, he looked for opportunities to work with crisis pregnancy centers and to tell his story to others. He was inspired by Proverbs 31:8-9: "Open your mouth for the mute, for the rights of all who are destitute. Open your mouth, judge righteously, defend the rights of the poor and needy."

Word spread as people heard Josiah's story. Invitations to speak multiplied. Everywhere he went, he shared the power of God's forgiveness, urging audiences to "find forgiveness so you can give forgiveness."

Today Josiah is a family pastor and pro-life advocate. His own adoption, he says, is a picture of how God adopts each one of us into His family. Josiah works with children, students, and families, helping others find their identity and value in the love of Jesus, affirming the value of every person created in the image of God, and proclaiming that His forgiveness has the power to transform the human heart.

12

THE VOICE: VANESSA'S STORY

Newborn Vanessa in the arms of her mother, Rasheedah

TWO DAYS AFTER RASHEEDAH CONCEIVED, her partner's mother died in his native home in Africa. Goodwin (her partner) had been in America on a student visa for nearly two years, yet his dream of attending dental school never materialized. Upon his mother's death, he decided to return home for good.

A few weeks later, when Rasheedah discovered she was pregnant, she contacted Goodwin. He made it clear: Not only was he not interested in having a child, but it would be bad luck to have a baby who wasn't planned. Having this child, he explained, would be against both his religion and his culture and would bring great shame to his family. Rasheedah's only option, he told her, was to have an abortion. Within days, money for the procedure appeared in her bank account.

As Rasheedah looked at her older boys, ages ten and fifteen, all she could think about was the difficulty of raising *three* children alone. She considered her options—one moment she agreed that abortion was the right choice given her circumstances. The next moment she sensed her heart saying no to the abortion. It was terribly stressful to be so evenly torn. She asked others for advice, but no one could tell her what she should do. No one said, "I think you should abort." Neither did anyone tell her, "Keep the baby. You can do it. We'll be there to support you."

Rasheedah was desperate for someone to help her make the choice and was upset that no one would. So she made an appointment at a Planned Parenthood clinic. When she arrived, some pro-life demonstrators approached her.

"You shouldn't go in that place," they said. "Please don't go in there." One of the demonstrators, a young man, told her, "Please call Maggie's Place. They can help you with whatever you need for your baby."

Rasheedah decided that perhaps she *should* go to Maggie's Place, a home for pregnant women. Despite her insistence that she didn't need somewhere to live, the young man told her that Maggie's Place could support her in whatever ways she needed—from the practical to the emotional. The people at Maggie's Place were very kind indeed. They welcomed Rasheedah and gave her a basket of baby supplies.

She was still very confused on the drive home. Just looking at the basket made her feel afraid. Even with support from the people at Maggie's Place, Rasheedah still couldn't imagine raising another baby on her own. Stress and anxiety took up residence in her mind, creating a heartrending tug-of-war.

She attempted to schedule another appointment with Planned Parenthood, but by this point their appointment slots had filled and they were now booked for weeks. Waiting that much longer would have allowed Rasheedah's pregnancy to proceed too far for a straightforward abortion. She eventually found an ob-gyn clinic that also performed abortions, and she scheduled her procedure.

A friend agreed to drive her to and from the clinic, but that friend never said whether she supported Rasheedah's decision to abort. She was just there to accompany her. The friend stayed in the waiting room with Rasheedah, and they both watched as post-abortive women emerged like zombies doped up on medication. When the nurse called Rasheedah's name, her friend promised that she would return for Rasheedah when called.

Rasheedah's exam included an ultrasound followed by a dose of misoprostol designed to soften her cervix for the procedure. When the doctor was ready for her, the clinic staff started prepping Rasheedah for the abortion. They gave her a sedative to calm her before the doctor began dilating her cervix with a series of metal rods used to open the cervix for removing the baby. Rasheedah felt out of it, but she could still detect certain sensations. Those sensations must have been painful, because she was vaguely aware of moaning throughout the process.

All of a sudden, Rasheedah heard a loud voice break through the fog and pain. The voice instructed her: "*Get up!*" Startled, she scooted away from the doctor and sat up.

"Stop—I can't do this!" Rasheedah said. *"Stop! I can't do this! STOP! I CAN'T DO THIS!"*

The doctor, nurse, and technician in the room all stared at her in shock. After a moment's hesitation, they urgently encouraged her to continue the procedure. Rasheedah was completely dilated at this point. If they stopped the abortion procedure now, they said, she was at very high risk of hemorrhage, miscarriage, or infection.

They nearly convinced Rasheedah, but she couldn't get the thought out of her mind: *Stop, I can't do this. Stop.* The feeling was overwhelming. She tried to come up with a good reason to go through with the abortion, but it was as if her brain had no room for anything other than *Stop!*

The doctor put down the cannula, and Rasheedah realized that she had stopped the doctor in the nick of time. The next step in the procedure was for the doctor to vacuum out her baby.

The doctor shook her head. "I've never stopped an abortion at this stage before," she said. "We really don't know what is going to happen."

The staff moved Rasheedah to recovery, monitored her, and performed a couple of ultrasounds to make sure the baby was still alive. As the sedative wore off, a hundred thoughts filled Rasheedah's mind. *What if something is wrong? What if this? What if that? Oh, you should finish it.* But it was too late. The clinic was closing. They weren't doing any more abortions that day. The staff checked her vitals and released her. Her ride had arrived; it was time to go home.

Once inside the car, Rasheedah's friend confided her suspicion. "I had a feeling that something was going to happen," she said, "and you wouldn't get the abortion."

Back home, Rasheedah continued to battle with her conflicting thoughts. *What do I do? What if I damaged the baby enough that it is going to have issues all its life?* For a moment she even tried jumping up and down. *Well, now that it's open, maybe the baby will fall out.*

Rasheedah was still bleeding and leaking amniotic fluid. Those physical issues, combined with Rasheedah's inner turmoil, prompted a trip to the emergency room. Once she reached the hospital, the questions that had plagued her since returning home tumbled out of her.

"There's nothing we can do for you right now," she was told. "You are just going to have to hope that everything will be okay."

Then they sent her home.

But home wasn't any better. It was agonizing to be there alone while her two older children were in school. Rasheedah had no one to talk to, no one to lean on. She'd thought the turmoil was bad before going to the clinic, but now it was even worse. Rasheedah now faced the added uncertainty of how badly she'd threatened her pregnancy. *What am I going to do now?* she thought. She paced around her two-bedroom apartment.

"I was a big mess," she says.

A TUG-OF-WAR

With no one to talk to, no one with whom she could process her actions and choices, Rasheedah waited only a few days before scheduling another abortion appointment with the same office. This time the clinic planned to perform the procedure under sedation because Rasheedah was so consumed by anxiety.

Rasheedah's mother was her ride this time. As they drove to the clinic, Rasheedah just stared out the window. Out of nowhere came a powerful nudge.

"I looked at my mom and said, 'Turn around,'" she recalls.

"As soon as I told her to turn around," Rasheedah says, "I experienced the most spiritual thing that has ever happened in my life. I felt complete peace."

Until that moment, Rasheedah was mired in stress and anxiety. *What do I do? Keep the baby or not?* Like an endless loop, the tug-of-war in her head raged on. But the moment they turned around, those overwhelming feelings instantly disappeared. Gone, like magic. Rasheedah can still remember the thoughts that replaced her fears: *Don't worry. You're going to be okay.*

While Rasheedah had faith that ultimately everything would be okay, she also knew that her pregnancy at that moment was definitely *not* okay. Just as the doctor had warned, her pregnancy was compromised from the day she halted her abortion.

The first ob-gyn she consulted seemed annoyed with her. He tried his best to be polite, but it was clear that he was completely against what she had done—especially when he heard that Rasheedah had made an appointment for a second abortion attempt. Because she continued to leak amniotic fluid, the doctor referred her to an office that specialized in high-risk pregnancies.

At this new practice, Rasheedah no longer felt judged, but remarkably cared for. There she learned two things: First, her baby was a girl. Second, the amniotic fluid surrounding her baby was dangerously low. Rasheedah was quickly educated on the complications that can arise when a baby lacks adequate amniotic fluid.

GOD WAS SPEAKING

When Rasheedah first heard that voice at the abortion clinic, she hadn't attributed it to God. But when she told others her story, they exclaimed, "That was God's voice!" The more she thought about it, the more she considered that what they said might be true. That realization made Rasheedah want to seek out what the Lord might have for her and her child.

Turning to God created a connection to Him in ways that Rasheedah had never experienced. She felt encouraged to pray, and she sensed God carrying her and protecting her even when she was hospitalized at nineteen weeks. Before the hospitalization, she had been quite stressed as a single mom raising her sons, going to work, and being pregnant alone. Normally, she would have seen an extended hospital stay as a huge negative that only added to her stress. Instead, she understood that God was giving her a time of rest. Over the following weeks and months, God gave Rasheedah a new perspective that changed her view from negative to grateful.

She began to focus her prayers on her unborn child. Rasheedah thought about how God had saved her daughter's life, and she wanted her daughter to embrace the characteristics of God. She wanted her child to have a higher purpose, to be someone who strove to fulfill God's desires for her. So every day she spoke to her unborn child: "I dedicate what is inside my womb to almighty God, to serve Him and to serve humanity."

As the doctors expected, Rasheedah developed an infection. Thus, her daughter was delivered at twenty-eight weeks. She weighed three pounds—considered a relatively good weight for that stage of gestation. Because of the lack of amniotic fluid surrounding her in the womb, the infant was born with one leg bent. She was also diagnosed with cerebral palsy and chronic lung disease. She spent the first three months of her life in the hospital.

"All because of the choice I made to abort her," Rasheedah says.

As of this writing, Rasheedah's daughter, Vanessa, is now ten years old. She still has health issues as a result of the abortion attempt and her premature birth. She can't run for long periods, she gets out of breath easily, and she is prone to lung infections, pneumonia, and the flu. But none of this stops her indomitable spirit. She may have physical limitations, but she is kind, loving, empathetic, and caring, and she has a great love for life and humanity. At age five, Vanessa told her mother, "I want to be like Martin Luther King Jr. and do what he did."

Curious, Rasheedah asked, "What did he do?"

"He made it so me and my friend Riley can sit together."

Nowadays, Vanessa says she wants to be president so that when she is in office, no one will be hungry or homeless.

Rasheedah attributes her daughter's special attributes to her prayers while Vanessa was still in her womb. Rasheedah has no doubt that as a result of surviving an abortion, Vanessa will do great things with her life through her desire to help humanity.

NO HAPPY ENDINGS

Rasheedah knows firsthand how it feels when a woman is considering abortion—not only because of her experience with Vanessa, but also because she actually has another abortion in her past. Her perspective was limited at the time of her earlier abortion, Rasheedah says, and she thought she was doing the right thing for herself and her circumstances. Her views have changed since then, and she wants to share what she's learned with other women who are now in that same situation.

"I understand why you think you want to have an abortion," she says. "But what you don't understand right now, and what no one is telling you, is that God's plans in this world go beyond what we can see."

Rasheedah says there are no happy endings with abortion, no matter the reasoning. To this day, she wonders what her life would look like now if she'd had that other baby. *What was down that path?* she asks herself. But she also realizes that she'll never know. And that realization—that *unknowing*—will stay with her for the rest of her life.

"That person had a right to be here," she says. "We need to remember that with abortion, we aren't only wiping out one person, we are wiping out generations of people to come. You don't know what they could have done to help this world. And you're never going to get away from that abortion. It's an empty spot inside you—a void that just grows and grows. I know God offers forgiveness, and He does forgive when we ask, but an abortion is never worth it."

It's quite clear to Rasheedah that although the clinics told her otherwise, Vanessa was always a *person*. A real person with a real purpose. She was meant to live, Rasheedah says, "and I should never have tried to take her life. She deserved to live then just as she deserves to live now. Babies deserve a chance to fulfill their life purpose."

Because she chose life for Vanessa, Rasheedah has since experienced God's presence on another level. She realized during her pregnancy that it was God who saved her daughter—and also saved her. While Vanessa was hospitalized for those three months, Rasheedah was impressed with the nurses who cared for them both. So she went back to school and became an obstetrics nurse herself. She also helps other women facing crisis pregnancies.

"I thought I was confused about my decision," Rasheedah says. "But the reality was, I was never confused. I was just making the wrong decision. *Life* was the right decision all along. That's why choosing life was the choice that finally brought me peace."

Two women from other countries later reached out to Rasheedah. Both wanted to abort their babies, but after hearing Rasheedah's story, both decided to keep their children instead. Rasheedah thought it was just her own baby she was saving when she heard a voice and sat up, so the knowledge that she is helping change minds halfway around the world gives her deep satisfaction.

Life was the right decision all along.

13

THE SECOND CHANCE: ZECHARIAH'S STORY

Zechariah with his mother, Rebekah

REBEKAH NEVER IMAGINED SHE'D HAVE AN ABORTION. Then again, she never imagined she would be pregnant at age seventeen *and again* at eighteen.

She was the fourth daughter born into a solid Christian family. They lived in a conservative, middle-class community in Placer County, California. The community was, and still is, beautiful, full of churches, good schools, and opportunities. There was one Planned Parenthood clinic in Placer County, but being tucked in the back of a business complex made it easy to hide and easy for residents to ignore.

Rebekah's three sisters were eight to sixteen years older than her. When she was eleven, one of her grown sisters died, upending Rebekah's predictable world and leaving behind two young daughters. Her parents adopted these two granddaughters, so Rebekah went from being the youngest of four girls to being the older sister of two toddlers. Rebekah's parents were no longer able to focus on guiding their youngest daughter to make good decisions. Instead, they were overwhelmed with grieving the loss of their older daughter while raising two little girls dealing with the trauma of losing their mother. It was all too much, and Rebekah began making unwise decisions.

By age fifteen, Rebekah had formulated a plan: finish high school with decent grades, go to college, begin a career. Her family didn't talk about boys, relationships, or sex, but Rebekah thought a lot about all of it. By sixteen, she had done more than just think. She met a boy who was three years older—technically a grown man—and began a relationship that eventually consumed her. By age seventeen, during the summer before her senior year of high school, she found out she was pregnant.

Rebekah was astounded. This wasn't supposed to happen to a girl like her—someone smart, from a solid home, with a solid life plan. Yet, like for so many "good girls" before her, it did.

Abortion never crossed her mind as an option. Instead, Rebekah thought she needed to be responsible and own up to the consequences of her behavior. She would adjust her senior year plans to include having a baby, naively thinking *It won't be that hard.*

Her parents, meanwhile, were shocked—especially her dad, who had more than a few choice words to say when he learned his daughter was expecting. He soon came around, though, and agreed to let Rebekah continue living at home. With her parents' help, she graduated high school six months early; gave birth to her son, Eli; turned eighteen; and immediately started classes at Sacramento State. Things were looking up, and her parents were proud of her.

But Rebekah was keeping a secret. Her relationship with her baby's father was abusive. In fact, he had been abusive toward her from the beginning. She has vivid memories of being seven months pregnant and using smoky eye shadow to make her left eye match her right—the one her partner had blackened and bruised. About six months into Rebekah's freshman year of college—which was also nearly six months into her new role as a mother—their relationship became increasingly violent. She no longer had only herself to worry about.

Rebekah was convinced that her son, although just an infant, was being negatively affected not only by the violence but also by her partner's affairs and his addictions to marijuana and pornography. She admitted to herself that she and her son were not safe in his presence and that she had to get out of the relationship. Yet Rebekah hesitated to tell her parents that the relationship had continued after her son's birth. She was afraid of letting them down again, but she desperately needed their support. Her parents were shocked by the news, yet they responded with grace and agreed to let her and Eli continue living in their home. Rebekah was deeply relieved. It was, after all, the only home she and her son had ever known.

However, there were conditions. In order to stay, she had to agree to three ground rules set by her parents. The first two rules were simple: "You won't have much of a social life" and "You need to stay in school." Now that Eli's father was out of the picture, the third rule seemed easy enough, though Rebekah's dad reminded her of it almost every time she left the house: "Don't you dare get pregnant again while you are living in this house."

He made it clear that if she did get pregnant, he would kick both her and Eli out. Rebekah's parents already had a lot on their plate with raising her little nieces, and they had done plenty to help her with Eli financially, emotionally, and physically. They simply didn't have the energy or resources to do it again.

Rebekah was grateful for this new start after her toxic relationship ended, but at the same time something was off, and she didn't quite know what. Although she didn't look or feel pregnant, and her cycle wasn't late, she decided to take a pregnancy test just to calm her mind and to make sure the loose ends from her past were truly severed.

The two-minute drive to the pharmacy set her nerves on edge. What if she ran into her parents, or her sisters who lived nearby and frequented the same store? Rebekah located the pregnancy tests, looking furtively up and down the aisle and hoping no one she knew was watching. After purchasing multiple tests, she headed straight for the store's restroom. As she sat alone in the cold public bathroom, two bright pink lines appeared in the pregnancy test window.

Positive.

Fear shot through her. This test had to be wrong. Rebekah ripped open a second package. Then a third. To her horror, all three were positive. That meant one thing: Her life was essentially over. She was just a month away from turning nineteen, and everything she had worked hard to achieve—not just for herself, but also for her ten-month-old son—ran through her mind.

There goes college. There go my dreams; my ability to provide for my son. What am I going to do?

Rebekah shivered as she recalled her dad's warning: "Don't you dare get pregnant . . ." She stared at those pink lines, blinking back the tears. Her swelling bubble of anxiety was about to burst. *There goes our home and stable family support. There go my son's daily needs—diapers and food. What am I going to do with two children? Two children from the same abusive dad, who is most certainly not going to be there for us! We're going to be alone, broke, and living in some run-down apartment.*

She exited the bathroom stall, wrapped the positive tests inside paper towels, and stuffed them in the trash. As she washed her hands, she could see the future clearly. *I'll be single forever, probably living off "the system," because there's no way anyone could love a mess like me.*

Stunned, Rebekah somehow made it back to her car. There she sat, staring into the distance. Her son didn't deserve this. Her parents didn't deserve this. Even her unborn child didn't deserve the life that awaited. She circled the block again and again, thinking, pondering, trying to sort out her options. But nothing came to her. If there were any options, they were beyond Rebekah's grasp.

AN EASY FIX?

She hadn't considered it at first, but perhaps there was a way out— a way to "fix" her problem pregnancy. The more Rebekah thought about it, the more she liked the idea: An abortion would spare her and everyone around her the shame, embarrassment, and hardship that another child would cause. An abortion could end this problem, quickly and quietly. No one would ever have to know, or suffer, except her. Her stomach tightened as she prayed, *God, You're just going to have to forgive me on this one.*

In her moment of crisis, an abortion looked like the "responsible" thing to do. The only compassionate choice for her, for the baby, for everyone involved. In this moment, Rebekah realized, an abortion looked a whole lot like hope.

But traditional surgical abortion procedures seemed frightening and invasive. Was there another option? A different way to handle this? She took out her phone and searched for "abortion options."

To Rebekah's relief, she learned that there was another way to quickly and easily undo the mess she'd gotten herself into. It was called a chemical/medical abortion, more commonly known as "the abortion pill." As far as she could tell, it really was just a pill. Simple. No big deal. A way to induce an abortion at about a third of the cost of a surgical procedure—which appealed to a young college freshman who wanted to hide this embarrassment from her family. Had a surgical abortion been her only option, Rebekah says, she probably wouldn't have chosen to terminate her pregnancy.

On March 13, 2013, she arrived for her appointment at a Planned Parenthood clinic in North Highlands, California. She was not yet eight weeks pregnant. Rebekah checked in, and after she had waited for what seemed like hours, an assistant called her name and escorted her to a back room. There she met a nurse with paperwork and two small Dixie cups. One held water. In the other cup was the first of two abortion pills.

"Are you sure you want to do this?" the nurse asked.

Rebekah nodded, but the nurse needed verbal confirmation, so Rebekah gave a quiet yes.

First box checked.

Rebekah took the cups and stared at the lone white pill. She began to tear up. The nurse calmly said, "You know, Rebekah, just because you're sad doesn't mean you're making the wrong decision."

She nodded and listened as the nurse proceeded to reiterate everything Rebekah had read online: "This will be very natural and will feel similar to your menstrual cycle. You'll take this first pill here in the office, and it's called mifepristone. Mifepristone ends your pregnancy. Once you take this, there is no going back.

Tomorrow, when you're ready, you'll take the second medication, misoprostol, which will expel the pregnancy."

It sounded simple enough. Like many almost-nineteen-year-olds, Rebekah didn't think to ask about the details of how it all worked. She didn't care. She just needed this to be over.

She lifted the medication cup to her lips, then the water. The nurse checked Rebekah's mouth to make sure she'd swallowed, handed her a bag with the misoprostol—the kind of brown paper bag kids pack their lunches in—and sent her on her way.

As Rebekah walked to her car, that four-ounce bag felt more like forty pounds, as it carried the weight of her unborn baby's life inside.

The moment she got to her car, she began to panic. *What did I just do? I don't even believe in abortion.*

Rebekah swallowed hard as she stared at the bag in her hand. *Has my baby already died? Did it feel pain?*

That's when she knew. She had just made the worst decision of her life, and all she could think to do was pray. Tears streamed down Rebekah's face. *God, if there is a way out of this, please help me find it,* she prayed. *And if not, please help me forgive myself.*

She grabbed her phone and instantly began searching for some way to undo her mistake. To her surprise, she was not alone. She read posts from other women asking the same question: "Can I stop a medication abortion after I've already started?" Unfortunately, the responses offered little hope: "You must finish what you started. Stopping now is dangerous."

Rebekah couldn't accept that answer. She kept scrolling and finally found an ad that encouraged women who had second thoughts after taking the abortion pill to call their hotline.

A kind nurse answered Rebekah's frantic call. The nurse asked questions that none of the clinic workers had: "Why did you choose abortion? What is your home life like? How do you feel now? Do you know how chemical abortion works?"

The nurse explained that the first pill, mifepristone, ends a pregnancy by starving the growing baby of the hormone essential for pregnancy—progesterone. The information surprised Rebekah, but there was even more she hadn't been told. The second drug, misoprostol—the one she was instructed to take the next day at home with no medical supervision—would induce labor. That same drug is also given to some women in labor to help soften the cervix and cause the uterus to contract, thus expelling the baby.

Rebekah was speechless. She was supposed to induce her own labor—at home over the toilet? Tears streamed down her face as she questioned why she had been underinformed and misled.

The nurse, however, did have some hopeful news to share. A doctor had recently helped a few women reverse their chemical abortions by prescribing progesterone to help counteract the progesterone-depriving mifepristone they'd taken. The nurse called it an abortion pill reversal.

"Are you willing to try?" she asked Rebekah. "I can't promise this will work, but it is a chance to save your baby."

"Yes! I'll do anything," Rebekah replied.

Less than twenty-four hours after taking the mifepristone abortion pill, Rebekah began progesterone treatment to try to save her baby. She stayed on the regimen for several weeks.

When the Planned Parenthood clinic called to see why she had never returned for her follow-up appointment—the one where they made sure that the "pregnancy" was expelled—she told them about her change of heart.

"Do you have any idea what you're doing?" the clinic worker asked.

Not really, Rebekah thought. *I'm just kind of living on a prayer here.*

"If you carry to term, which isn't likely, your baby could potentially have severe fetal anomalies," the worker said.

Those words were the last ones Rebekah ever heard from an organization she had trusted with the biggest decision of her life. At the time, she could not understand why they so desperately wanted her to finish what she had started in their clinic. There was no "Let us know what happens" or "Call us back if you change your mind." There was nothing.

Planned Parenthood's frightening words haunted her for the remaining seven months of her pregnancy. Rebekah was convinced she would lose the baby, or that it would be born with an ailment that she'd have to tell everyone—including her child—was due to her abortion attempt.

Thankfully, Planned Parenthood was wrong.

Also thankfully, Rebekah's parents—after careful consideration—extended grace and allowed her to continue living in their home.

On October 20, 2013, Rebekah welcomed another baby boy into her life. She was so grateful for God's goodness that she named him Zechariah, which means "the Lord remembers." Zechariah was, and still is, perfectly healthy. He is bright and charismatic, and he dreams of being a movie director. Even before he was ten, Zechariah knew the age-appropriate truth about his story, as he has heard his mother recount it many times. But he does not yet know or understand the word *abortion*. He knows that sometimes, when pregnant mommies get scared and need help, they make poor decisions. He knows that was his mother's experience too, and that a doctor helped save him while he was still in her tummy.

Rebekah completed her college education, graduating in 2017. She now works for Heartbeat International, where she raises awareness and funds for pregnancy centers and the Abortion Pill Rescue Network. Since 2015, God has used her to help influence others via pregnancy center events, Christian conferences, and pro-life rallies. Her story has been featured on VICE News, HBO, and Focus on the Family, among other outlets. She has testified in favor of pro-life legislation and informed consent laws in various states, helping women become better informed about abortion pill reversal.

While Rebekah never thought she'd get an abortion, she also never thought—not in a million years—that she'd make the transformation from reckless teenage mom to someone who addresses high-level leaders. While it's a wonderful opportunity to be a part of these events, Rebekah knows that her true value comes from Christ. She is redeemed. Just a sinner saved by grace.

Like so many others, she is a woman who bought the lie that abortion is an easy way out of a bad situation; yet she is also one who received a second chance to choose life. God took her from *reckless* to *rescued*.

"It is so neat," Rebekah says, "to see how He has taken this messy story and made it His beautiful message."

To date, more than three thousand babies have been saved thanks to abortion pill reversal.[1] Rebekah was told by her doctor that Zechariah was among the first. Thankful as she is for her second son, Rebekah is sad that so many women are still misled into thinking that medical abortions are simple, quick, convenient— and irreversible.

"My hope is to share the news that women do not need abortion to succeed," she says, "that babies don't end dreams, and that a life better than you can imagine is waiting on the other side of your yes to God."

14

PIVOTAL MOMENTS: JILL'S STORY

Jill Stanek

WHEN JILL STANEK ARRIVED AT CHRIST HOSPITAL in Oak Lawn, Illinois, for her night shift as a labor and delivery nurse, there was no indication that this night would drastically alter her life. Only God knew she'd be sitting in a recovery room comforting a tiny, unwanted infant—born alive after an attempted abortion—until he took his last breath. In the days that followed, when it would have been easier to look the other way, Jill's commitment to Christ led her to risk her job, reputation, and friendships by opposing not only the terrible practice of abortion but of infanticide as well.

Since Jill is a nurse and not an abortion survivor, you might wonder why I am including her story in this book. As you learn about her experience, I believe you'll discover the ways in which Jill is simply another kind of survivor. You will see how Jill's actions threatened her status, her reputation, and her career. Instead of looking the other way, Jill broke her silence and became a champion for life.

That evening at Christ Hospital in the late 1990s wasn't the first time an encounter with a dying baby triggered a transformation in Jill. As a twenty-year-old, Jill was driving along a familiar highway when she became the first person to arrive at the scene of a terrible car accident, and that tragic event birthed a new passion within her.

A car containing four adults and a baby had been rear-ended by a semitruck. The baby's father was clearly in shock as he sat next to the crushed car, holding his dying child. Jill ran up to help but didn't know what to do.

"I remember feeling very helpless as I watched that baby dying," Jill says, "and I remember saying to myself that I never wanted to feel that way again."

After her youngest child entered the first grade, Jill enrolled at South Suburban College in South Holland, Illinois, with the goal of becoming a nurse. She graduated in 1993 and began her nursing career at Christ Hospital in suburban Chicago—a facility Jill chose specifically because it was a Christian hospital. She spent two years gaining experience in the cardiac telemetry ward before transferring to the specialty she'd always wanted—labor and delivery.

At every shift change, the incoming staff gathered for a status report on their assigned patients as well as any upcoming procedures scheduled to take place in their department. During one particular status report, Jill learned that a doctor would be aborting a second-trimester baby with Down syndrome using an induced-labor abortion procedure.

Also known as a "live-birth abortion," this method is sometimes used to abort second- and third-trimester babies. Doctors do not attempt to terminate the baby in the uterus but instead force a premature delivery so that the baby dies during the birth process or soon afterward. The small, fully formed baby is sometimes delivered alive—at which point it is left to die. Furthermore, not all these babies have an illness or deformity. Some of these procedures are performed on otherwise healthy babies.

Jill was shocked that this procedure was on the schedule. She had wanted to work at this hospital because she presumed that a Christian hospital would not perform abortions. The hurt cut especially deep with Jill because the hospital was named after her Lord and Savior, Jesus Christ.

Later that night, after the abortion procedure was complete, one of Jill's coworkers took the still-breathing infant to a utility room. His parents didn't want to hold him while he died, and the nurse didn't have time. Jill, however, couldn't bear the thought of this suffering child dying alone. "So," she says, "I cradled and rocked him for the forty-five minutes that he lived."

As she held this tiny boy who weighed about eight ounces at twenty-one weeks' gestation, Jill felt as though she had stepped outside herself. She couldn't believe this was happening. "It was so surreal—made even more so because this was a hospital with *Christ* in its name!"

After the child was pronounced dead, Jill folded his little arms across his chest, wrapped him in a tiny shroud, and carried him to the hospital morgue where all dead patients were taken.

THE TRUTH COMES OUT

When Jill shared her experience with others, it wasn't long before more stories came out, and Jill decided to embark on an informal investigation of her own.

One associate recounted cleaning a utility room where she picked up a towel someone had left on the counter. As she tossed it into the laundry bin, she realized someone had wrapped a still-alive aborted baby in the linens. Horrified, she dug through the trash until she found the baby. As she tried to remove it from the garbage, however, the baby fell out of the towel and onto the floor.

Other aborted babies were found alive in Christ Hospital's utility rooms, either naked on a scale or on the metal counter. In an unusual case, one of these babies lived for almost an entire eight-hour shift.

Some patients had no idea that their babies could be born alive following an induced abortion. One particular mother didn't want to hold her child, but after he was taken to the utility room, she kept asking, "Is he dead yet? Is he dead yet?"

A fellow nurse told Jill about another patient who didn't realize that her baby might survive the abortion. The mother and father were not only shocked when their little boy was born alive, but they were also surprised that the infant didn't have the external physical deformities they had been warned about.

The mother screamed for someone to help her baby, and the nurse rushed to call a neonatologist. But after the neonatologist examined the baby, he said that there was nothing he could do because the little guy had been born too early. The mother was so traumatized that she had to be given a tranquilizer. The baby was tenderly held by his grandmother for the half hour that he lived.

Then there was the nurse who attended an induced-labor abortion for a baby diagnosed, via ultrasound, with spina bifida. During the procedure, however, the boy emerged with an intact spine. What looked like spina bifida in the ultrasound images was actually an incompletely formed twin that appeared as a mass on his brother's back. The father came to the utility room to see his son, saw that he had been involved in aborting a completely healthy baby, and then left the room without a word.

Another nurse, who was about twenty-three weeks pregnant at the time, assisted a patient who was also twenty-three weeks along but was unable to carry her child to term. The baby herself was healthy, but at twenty-three weeks' gestation, she had only about a 39 percent chance of survival. If the mother had wanted to fight for her daughter's life, a team of specialists would have attended the delivery, ready to whisk the baby to the NICU for specialized care. But the mother chose abortion instead.

Thus the only hospital staff present for the abortion were an obstetrical resident and the pregnant nurse. After the procedure, the baby girl, who showed signs of thriving, was merely wrapped in a blanket and kept in the labor and delivery area until she died two and a half hours later.

"I can't stop thinking about it," the attending nurse said.

Just three weeks after that baby was aborted, another mother came to the hospital under similar circumstances and was offered the same options. But this mother said that she wanted her baby to live. This time the NICU team *was* present at her delivery, and this time the little girl survived.

After Jill's experience holding the tiny boy while he died, then learning of so many other stories, the weight of what was happening in her hospital became too much to bear. She decided that she had two choices: The first option was to quietly leave Christ Hospital for someplace that didn't perform abortions. The other was to challenge Christ Hospital's abortion practices.

While wrestling with this dilemma, Jill read a passage in *The Living Bible* that spoke to her and her situation: "Rescue those who are unjustly sentenced to death; don't stand back and let them die. Don't try to disclaim responsibility by saying you didn't know about it. For God, who knows all hearts, knows yours, and he knows you knew! And he will reward everyone according to his deeds" (Proverbs 24:11-12, TLB).

"I decided that to quit at that point would be irresponsible and actually disobedient to God," Jill says. "Sure, I might be more comfortable if I left the hospital, but babies would continue to die."

Though she didn't know it at the time, Jill's decision would lead to additional hurt as she learned more about the practice of allowing babies born alive after induced-labor abortions to be left alone to die. But the same God who uses everything for our good and His glory also used Jill's pain as a catalyst for change and to make clear her calling. What she discovered along the way was both distressing and discouraging, but instead of paralyzing her, the information spurred her to action.

AN ADVOCATE FOR LIFE

Jill wrote a letter to the Christ Hospital administration describing her experience with the aborted and dying child, certain that they couldn't possibly know about this barbaric practice. To her dismay, she learned that they did know. Two department superiors called her in for a meeting, telling her that they considered induced-labor abortion the most compassionate procedure because it allows parents an opportunity to hold their baby as he or she dies. This, they said, was better for both mother and baby. It also allows parents to gain closure and to grieve properly as they can see their dead baby. They told Jill it would be a shame to lose her, but perhaps she might be better suited to working at a hospital that shared her pro-life convictions.

But Jill had no intention of quitting. Walking away, she thought, would make her just another Christ Hospital victim of abortion. No, she had not yet done enough to oppose the abortions taking place at the hospital named after her Savior.

So Jill consulted with her pastor, and together they determined the next step was to alert some pro-life organizations and individuals and ask them to help privately. Two of these individuals were Dr. C. Everett Koop, the former US surgeon general, and Cardinal Francis George, the archbishop of Chicago. Both men wrote to Christ Hospital condemning its abortion practice and asking that it stop.

More investigating from Jill and others revealed that the procedures at Christ Hospital—affiliated with the Evangelical Lutheran Church of America and the United Church of Christ, both abortion-affirming denominations—did not violate any state laws. However, the hospital's parent company, Advocate Health Care, soon revised its policies to no longer permit abortions of fetuses with nonlethal birth defects like Down syndrome or spina bifida.

Since private appeals had done little to deter the hospital, Jill's pastor wrote a letter in July 1999 to seventy pro-life organizations and churches telling them about Christ Hospital and its abortion practices. It was this letter that brought local and national attention to the hospital. Before Jill knew it, the story appeared in *Newsweek* and the *New York Times* and on television shows like *The O'Reilly Factor*.

In June 2001, a bill known as the Born-Alive Infants Protection Act was introduced in the US House of Representatives. The bill affirmed that any baby born alive after an abortion attempt has the same legal rights and protections as you and I. Jill testified many times on behalf of the bill, in both oral and written form, before the US House Judiciary Subcommittee on the Constitution as well as before state legislative committees in Illinois, Colorado,

Michigan, and Wisconsin. Her testimony was also read on multiple occasions during key congressional debates of abortion legislation. (It is worth noting that her public testimony has never been denied or refuted by Christ Hospital.)

In the midst of the national publicity, congressional hearings, state investigations, prayer vigils, and picket protests, Jill continued to work at Christ Hospital for another two and a half years. She didn't like staying, but as she read the Bible and prayed, she never felt the freedom to leave. Isaiah 8:17-18 kept coming back to her: "I will wait for the LORD. . . . I will wait for Him. Here I am with the children the LORD has given me" (HCSB).

Even before Jill blew the whistle regarding abortion survivors at her hospital, an aborted baby who was born alive was supposed to receive "comfort care." Jill describes this as wrapping the baby in a blanket and offering him or her to the parents to hold until the baby died. If parents did not want to hold their baby (as Jill observed was often the case), caring for the baby was left to staff. If no one was available, the baby was taken to a utility room to die alone.

FREE TO SPEAK

In December 2000, not long after Jill began speaking out, Christ Hospital unveiled a comfort room. No longer did nurses take live aborted babies to the utility room, but rather to this small, nicely decorated room with a wooden rocker to rock the babies while they were dying. Amenities included equipment to take photos, baptismal supplies, and even a foot printer and baby bracelets for parents who wanted keepsakes of their child. A comfort room can't undo what's been done, but it is a step toward treating these tiny humans with dignity and compassion.

It was only after Jill took photos of the comfort room that Christ Hospital finally fired her in August 2001, citing that act as one of the reasons for her termination. The other reasons related to her public outspokenness against the hospital's abortion practices. Her termination meant Jill was completely free to discuss her experiences. Here's what happened as a result:

- On August 5, 2002, President George W. Bush invited Jill to his signing of the Born-Alive Infants Protection Act, which defines children who survive an abortion attempt as people who deserve the same medical care as any other baby.
- On November 5, 2003, President Bush invited Jill to his signing of the Partial-Birth Abortion Ban Act, which protects partially delivered babies from being killed by abortion.
- On June 4, 2009, MSNBC commentator Keith Olbermann named Jill the "Worst Person in the World" for her pro-life advocacy—a badge of honor she proudly wears.
- In 2015, the Family Research Council awarded Jill the Digital Pro-Life Pioneer Award for her pro-life blogging.
- Also in 2015, Jill joined the Susan B. Anthony List as national campaign chair, working to elect pro-life leaders to office.
- In June 2020, Jill accepted a position as community outreach manager with the Pregnancy and Life Assistance Network.

As the media covered Jill's story time and time again, they continued to characterize induced-labor abortions as rare. Yet there are still thousands of such abortions each year, so it is not as rare as some would like us to believe. Indeed, the practice is common at hospitals across the nation.

Making the public aware of the procedure was only the beginning.

"The journey God has taken me on since I first stepped out in obedience to fight abortion at a hospital named after His Son has been overwhelming!" Jill says. "I traveled around the country describing what I and other staff have witnessed. . . . The subject of Christ Hospital and live-birth abortion garnered much public attention. Descriptions of live-birth abortions have now been told on national television, on radio, in print, and by local and national legislators, instead of simply being practiced in the dark."

Gabriel Gene Stanek, Jill's first grandson, arrived on August 12, 2000, and through his birth, God brought the issue of extremely premature birth into sharp focus. Gabriel was born fifteen weeks premature, at a gestational age of only twenty-five weeks. When Jill got the call from her son, she and her husband rushed to the hospital to see their two-pound grandchild.

"The first thing that struck me," Jill says, "was that Gabriel was so premature that his eyes were still fused shut."

She was instantly transported back to a time in Christ Hospital's NICU when a neonatologist tried to make the case that sometimes "we save babies we shouldn't save." Jill says the doctor pointed out one such premature baby to help demonstrate his point.

"He took the little baby's head in his hand and turned it toward me. He said, 'See, Jill, this baby's eyes are still fused shut. This is a sign that this baby was too young to save.'"

Jill could only thank God that Gabriel was born in a hospital that fought to save *all* lives. Indeed, Gabriel is now a thriving young adult and is the joy of his family.

Jill never viewed herself as capable or qualified to embark

on the battle she's fought all these years—one that began with a prayer, a verse, and a step toward obedience. Not only did God equip her, but He has also been with her each step of the way, leading her and creating opportunities she never anticipated. If Jill—who began her journey with a simple act of kindness and compassion to a dying baby—could make such a difference just by being obedient, then so can others.

Jill says she can personally testify that "each one of us has a voice that we must use to stop the atrocity of abortion."

15

NO MORE SECRETS

Dr. Stephen Hammond

EVERY SURVIVOR IN THIS BOOK EXPERIENCED a moment in life that changed everything. For Jill Stanek, it was comforting a dying infant. For Dr. Stephen Hammond,[1] that moment was the surprise of a tiny baby's kick.

Steve Hammond was raised in a Christian home. His mother, the spiritual leader of the family, introduced him to Jesus at such an early age that Steve can't remember a time when he didn't know Him. Yet by the time he went off to college, Steve had compartmentalized that aspect of his life, separating his faith from his life choices.

Steve was a young medical school resident in 1973 when the faculty and mentoring doctors gathered the students to tell them about a so-called advancement in reproductive health for

women: the US Supreme Court's decision in *Roe v. Wade*. Steve
didn't think much about it, and thus his unwitting indoctrination
began. Moreover, his mind was already consumed with his studies,
his wife, and their newborn child—as well as their tight financial situation. In those days, a hospital resident's salary was barely
enough to cover necessities for a stay-at-home wife and a newborn,
and the school bills kept piling up. Like many other residents,
Steve worked other jobs to help make ends meet.

In April 1974, he was assigned to an abortion rotation during which he was introduced to the procedure. Residents weren't
required to perform abortions and were even allowed to opt out
of this rotation. Yet like many young doctors, Steve did not opt
out, and he became quite good at performing abortions. In fact,
he believed that he'd found his moneymaking niche.

The chance to make even more money prompted Steve to
travel to multiple abortion clinics. Wherever he went, the clinic
workers made it easy for doctors like Steve to do their work quickly
and efficiently. The staff met with patients in advance and prepped
them on procedure day. All Steve had to do was show up and
perform the abortions.

In those days clinics didn't have ultrasound machines, so
patients depended on the staff to accurately determine the gestational age of the preborn baby. This was usually calculated by asking questions, taking a patient's history, and performing a careful
physical examination.

One Saturday morning, a year and a half after he'd started
moonlighting at a Planned Parenthood clinic, Steve began an abortion procedure on the last patient of the morning. She was a bit
overweight, so it had been difficult for the nurse to complete a
thorough physical exam.

"I knew something was wrong right away," Steve recalls. "Usually there are a few teaspoons or tablespoons of amniotic fluid. This time, amniotic fluid was pouring and pouring.

"We even had to change the canister," he says, referring to the container in which the amniotic fluid (and, in the case of abortion, the parts of the baby) collected.

At that moment, the unthinkable happened.

"The baby kicked me!" he says.

Steve realized that they were in big trouble. He immediately did a more thorough examination and determined that this baby probably weighed three pounds. For the abortion to continue, the mother had to be transported to a hospital for a dismemberment abortion. So she was.

By this time, Steve had performed approximately seven hundred abortions. After each procedure, he routinely went through the parts of the baby piece by piece, like a pathologist during an autopsy. (This practice is meant to ensure that all body parts are accounted for and none were left in the mother's body.) He typically completed this task in a clinical manner, but this baby's kick triggered an awakening in Steve's spirit. His conscience was stirred, and he became convinced that every abortion involved the taking of life. In that moment, he decided he was done.

Yet he continued to refer patients for abortions.

A number of years later, Steve and his wife had their last child—a boy born at twenty-six weeks who weighed two pounds and three ounces.

"This awakened me once again," he says, "that while doctors were trying to save my child at this gestation, other doctors were ending the lives of children at his same gestation."

Dr. Stephen Hammond's moment had come. He never referred

a woman for abortion again. He could have remained silent about his past as an abortionist. He could have kept his story a secret and quietly moved on. But he didn't. He started speaking out.

"Abortion is not an amoral, abstract concept," he says. "It is the violent, gruesome destruction of a baby. Most Americans would oppose abortion if they observed one."

He wants others to experience the same awakening he did—to feel that baby's kick.

SHARING STORIES, EXPOSING SECRETS

Abortion survivors, their families, maternity nurses like Jill, and even clinic workers and former abortionists like Steve could all keep their abortion stories to themselves. They could decide to carry those untold stories quietly, privately. People must weigh their reasons for choosing whether to share such personal experiences, and I respect those reasons. But I also believe that abortion thrives in secret.

As illustrated throughout this book, survivors' life stories are often shrouded in secrets. Most of those secrets are intended to protect survivors from the pain of knowing their stories. But no matter how well intentioned, those same secrets can inflict even more pain as well as hinder healing. Yes, uncovering our stories can cause pain—for both ourselves and for others—but along with the pain of truth comes the freedom of understanding. Understanding difficult family dynamics. Understanding abuse and neglect. Understanding the physical, emotional, mental, and spiritual suffering that survivors experience. And understanding those truths is what ultimately sets us on a path toward healing.

Many voices, however, want to silence all of us who have an abortion story to tell. They say that speaking the truth about abortion is hateful and hurtful. I disagree. When done with compassion and care, sharing the truth is among the most loving things we can do. We have spoken the truth in this book, no matter how difficult it was, because we care enough to break our silence and expose our secrets.

The rest of the world deserves to know the truth about failed abortions and the existence of survivors. This is one way to create a culture of life: no more secrets. Bring the truth to light. The more we acknowledge these experiences, the more people impacted by abortion will break their silence. That's why I'm grateful to Steve, Jill, and all the survivors who allowed me to share their stories with you.

The healing and support offered at ASN begins with sharing our stories. And sharing our stories requires us to find and use our voices. I've seen in my own life and work that having a voice goes hand in hand with healing. And using those voices to tell our stories can have a positive impact—on ourselves, on our loved ones, and on our culture.

I trust that these stories of survival have shed new light on the humanity of the unborn and have provided a glimpse into the reality of failed abortions. The lives of survivors are not, as some claim, fabrications or some sort of political stunt. Nor is this book a work of fiction. Others like us continue to be born alive—even to this day. In fact, as I'm writing this, I know of an infant who recently survived a late-term abortion after his mother stopped the procedure when it became too painful. As a result he was born prematurely. Will his story someday be shared openly?

My sincerest hope and prayer is that survivors and their families are supported to the extent that they never doubt their inherent value, that they know they're not alone in their experiences, and that they can share their stories with confidence.

As you've now learned, survivors have often suffered in shame,

ABORTION SURVIVORS BREAK THEIR SILENCE

silence, and isolation. Our healing is further complicated by the secrets and hurts within our families, often very broken themselves. Even more complications arise because of the marginalization and stigmatization of abortion survivors—the fact that survivors have been declared nonexistent by our culture, mainstream media, and politicians. When these things are taken as a whole, you begin to understand why we've long kept our secrets to ourselves.

This book is my shout-out to the world and my appeal to you that the days of keeping our very existence a secret are over. We are stepping out of the shadows and into the light for all to see. But don't let our seemingly sudden appearance lead you to believe that abortion survivors are somehow a new phenomenon. You now know that just as abortion has existed throughout time, so, too, have abortion survivors.

THE RIPPLE EFFECT

A culture that embraces abortion is a culture that fails women. Our culture failed Rebekah when she took her first abortion pill. Our culture failed Priscilla when she believed that an abortion was the only way to keep her boyfriend. Our culture has failed unborn children, and it has failed survivors of abortion. When the solution to life's difficulties and uncertainties is the taking of life, then the culture has failed us all.

Surviving abortion has a lasting impact—not only on survivors but also on their biological parents, adoptive parents, siblings, adoption workers, doctors, and nurses. Abortion then has a ripple effect that includes children born to abortion survivors and beyond.

Abortion is a thief. It steals not just lives but generations. It causes immeasurable suffering. No matter the procedure, no matter the circumstances, the mere act of abortion is the deliberate taking of a human life. Every life has dignity and value, meaning and purpose. Instead of throwing up our collective hands and saying "Abortions have always existed, so we should just accept it," why don't we instead ask what we can do to *prevent* women from feeling compelled to even consider this decision? As pro-life writer Frederica Mathewes-Green so powerfully stated, "No one wants an abortion as she wants an ice-cream cone or a Porsche. She wants an abortion as an animal, caught in a trap, wants to gnaw off its own leg."[2]

Abortion isn't a sign that women are free, but a sign that they are desperate.

So how can we turn the tide and shape a world where women are supported and abortion is unthinkable? How do we get there?

We get there by being like Jill Stanek.

We get there by being like Stephen Hammond.

We get there by being like the nurse that rushed me off to the NICU.

We get there by listening to and sharing the stories of survivors.

STORIES INSPIRE HOPE

While every survivor's experience is different, the tie that binds our lives and our stories together is *hope*. Hope for a future. Hope for a society where life is valued. Hope for a family where one truly belongs, where all are loved and wanted. In the midst of the pain and the secrets, there is always hope. Just look at the survivors! Look at Rebekah and Rasheedah and Mica. Our culture might insist that abortion empowers women, but we know better. It is *hope* that empowers women. Hope fosters restoration and reconciliation. Hope inspires love and compassion. Hope leads to healing, love, and forgiveness.

You know what inspires hope? Stories of survival like the ones collected here! Each one demonstrates that human life can triumph over the bleakest of circumstances. We survivors have hope for a different world, a better world. We know that where there is life, there is hope. We are living proof of that.

HOPE INSPIRES ACTION

As I've reflected on my life, I've come to recognize the vital position I'm in and the platform I've been given. As a survivor, I discovered that I'm not nearly as alone as I previously believed. I saw how telling my story and sharing my experiences helped other survivors make an impact. I knew I had to do more, but I had no idea back then what more would look like! I just couldn't sit back and wait for someone else to speak up. And by taking action, I discovered new opportunities—to hear stories like mine, to forge relationships with other survivors and their families, to discern new ways to have a positive impact.

Therein lies the lesson: We can always do *something*. Just as the survivors and family members mentioned in this book put their compassion into action, we also recognize there is always *more* to be done. Sometimes it's simply a matter of stepping up and investing ourselves.

We get there by putting our belief in the dignity and value of *every* life into action. And when our beliefs are shaped by love, the results are *transformative*. My parents, who put their love into action through adoption, essentially loved me into life!

The dying baby that Jill Stanek comforted at Christ Hospital was a survivor, if only for an hour. Although his life was all too short, his story lives on through Jill's story. Because Jill put her beliefs into action that day, demonstrating compassion to a tiny, frail fellow human being, he experienced love in his brief time alive. Although his circumstances were tragic, he made an indelible mark on this world: His death was a defining moment in Jill's life, and that moment motivated her to take further action.

Jill's response serves as a model for the rest of us—an example of how our beliefs, shaped by love, can lead to action. Few of us will ever encounter a child left to die after an abortion, but we can all do *something*.

"I realize not everyone can just jump in feet first like I did," Jill wrote in her blog.

We're not all supposed to be like Jill. We don't all have to jump into the deep end. But we can all dip our toes in the water.

ACTION CHANGES LIVES

So where to begin? What's the best way to put love into action? Well, the easiest place to start is with those around us. We all encounter women in crisis, or men struggling to support a girl-friend or wife facing an unplanned pregnancy. Whether you realize it or not, our churches are filled with hurting people who have been impacted by abortion—women and men who desperately need to hear that they aren't alone in their suffering, that there is hope and forgiveness and healing to be found. (For specific ideas on how to help, see Appendix A: So You Want to Make a Difference?)

Stories like the ones in this book continue to unfold around us. Stories featuring women who, through circumstance or coercion, feel that abortion is the only answer. They need our compassion, so be ready to share it.

And what does compassion look like?

Compassion is speaking the truth in love about abortion and survivors. Compassion means coming alongside people who need support and healing after an abortion. Compassion also comes in the form of organizations like pregnancy centers. (Learn more in Appendix B: Resources.) Pregnancy centers provide services such as ultrasounds, STI testing, prenatal care, and parenting classes, plus material assistance like clothing, diapers, and more—usually free of charge. These centers are safe places for women to discuss all the options they're considering, free from the pressures they'd likely face at an abortion clinic.

This brings me to another way to get involved: adoption support. While some pregnancy centers offer in-house services for women considering adoption for their child, most centers have working relationships with outside adoption agencies and other support organizations.

Although it often involves emotional difficulties for all members of the adoption triad (biological parents, adoptive parents, and adoptees), adoption builds families and contributes to a culture of life. Adoption can also be a burden. Birth parents deserve and need support, as do adoptees and adoptive parents. Whether working with an established organization or simply helping out as a friend, supporting adoptive (as well as foster care) families is a great way to put compassion into action.

A CULTURE IN NEED

After reading these personal accounts of survival, I hope you believe, as I do, that what happens to a baby who has just survived an abortion attempt should never be left solely in the hands of the abortionist or a mother in an emotionally distressed state. In other words, a survivor's treatment and care should never depend on who happens to be in the clinic that day.

I'm going to repeat that: *A survivor's treatment and care should never depend on who happens to be in the clinic that day.*

Our culture is in desperate need of laws that uphold the dignity and value of life, including additional "born-alive" legislation that includes *consequences* for failing to provide medical care for abortion survivors. I've worked with several courageous lawmakers who are great examples of putting pro-life compassion into action, using their positions to do more, and refusing to remain silent in a world that views abortion as a right and supports it as the status quo.

These are just a few ways to get involved, but please don't limit yourself to these examples. Be creative. Ask God for guidance and opportunities. Our world needs more compassion—motivated by love and put into action.

CHANGED LIVES TRANSFORM THE WORLD

Truth be told, I wish I didn't have to write a book like this; I've only done so because children are still being aborted. But until that changes, I want there to be more stories told about abortion survivors. I want them alive to tell their own stories, which means they received proper medical care and were not left alone to die.

I have a dream for this book—that an outpouring of action will flow from people reading these stories. If your perspective has altered and your understanding has grown, then your life is no longer the same. And changed lives lead to transformed societies. Every survivor in this book has helped shape their world, and you can do the same.

Let's heal together. Let's break the silence in our families. Let's raise our collective voices. Let's not hesitate to confront media outlets that bury or even ignore stories about survivors, about post-abortive men and women, or about medical professionals and clinic workers who've seen the truth about abortion—all of whom threaten the predominant media narrative. Finally, let's hold our legislators accountable for their actions, making sure to thank and encourage those who support and respect life.

It's time to do away with secrets. In their place, it *is* time to have difficult conversations about past choices and painful experiences. Supporting abortion survivors and their families begins with understanding the circumstances that drive birth mothers to consider abortion. Demonstrating love and compassion for everyone involved is another important step. Take what you've learned from this book and apply it to your thoughts, your conversations, and—most importantly—your interactions with others.

How different would our culture look if the truth were told—if survivors were acknowledged and supported instead of discredited and ridiculed? How different would our world look if we acknowledged the impact of abortion and our need for healing? How different would our society look if we spoke of abortion openly and respectfully, not in hushed whispers or angry arguments?

Together, our voices will be amplified. I hope you will add your voice to those you read about in these pages. As Nobel Peace Prize winner Malala Yousafzai so beautifully stated, "We realize the importance of our voice when we are silenced."[3]

It is time for abortion survivors to break their silence!

APPENDIX A

So You Want to Make a Difference?

IT'S MY HOPE THAT THIS BOOK has stirred a fire within you to make a difference in the lives of those who have already been impacted by abortion and of those who remain vulnerable to abortion. I hope you've also discovered encouragement and inspiration for your own life in terms of perseverance, healing, finding your voice, forgiving, and loving others.

We've only begun to scratch the surface in terms of finding existing abortion survivors. The winds of change are upon us when it comes to abortion, as evidenced by the overturning of *Roe v. Wade* that occurred while this book was being written. But as you've learned through these survivors' stories, babies survived abortion before *Roe v. Wade*, they survived while *Roe v. Wade* was in effect, and they are continuing to survive today—after abortion legislation was returned to individual states following *Roe*'s reversal. The need to support women and families is as great as ever. As survivors' stories come to light, we must give them and their families the time and resources they need in order to heal and find their voices.

I take great hope in knowing that we can all help make a difference. Advocating for life is never a hopeless cause. And where there is life, there is hope.

Your life is part of that hope.

Just as every abortion survivor has a distinctly unique story, you, too, have distinct gifts, interests, and circumstances—a diverse set of experiences, skills, and passions that you can use to help support and advance the pro-life movement.

So how can you make a difference? The first step is to accept that you—yes, you—are a valuable person who *can* advocate for change. I can't tell you how many times I've heard people diminish their value because they don't have an "important" calling or a unique life experience, but the truth is that you need not have been subjected to an abortion attempt to help make a difference.

In other words, you are worthy, you are capable, and you do have what it takes. Don't get caught up in what someone else is doing or in comparing your impact with that of others. Instead, focus on your strengths and what you can do.

"But Melissa, I don't even know what I'm good at!"

Perhaps you don't, but there are lots of tools out there to help you assess your strengths and talents. Take some time to discover what you're passionate about. Appendix B is a great resource if you're looking for help from a pro-life organization, but it's also a great way to find places that you can serve with your time, your talents, or your financial support. You may be gifted with more time than talent, or more talent than time. Maybe you have the ability to make a difference financially. Fulfilling *your* calling, whatever it might be, is what's really important. There are many ways you can make a difference, even from the comfort of your home!

WAYS TO MAKE A DIFFERENCE

Have the difficult conversations. I'm not talking about conversations in public forums or on social media. I'm talking about discussions with the people you already know—your family, friends, and church community. If we want to move toward healing and reconciliation, then we need to be honest with ourselves and our loved ones about abortion and its impact in our lives.

As tough as it can be to talk about one's experience with abortion, something beautiful takes place when we bring the pain of abortion to light and work to find freedom from that pain. Preparing for these conversations takes time, but it's worth it.

Heal. Healing is often a long and complicated process. It's not linear, and it's never fully complete. Life happens, and more losses and trauma occur. Life happens, and you recognize the fallout from past hurts and misguided choices. Almost every day, I still experience transformation as I heal from past wounds. The same goes for my colleagues in other healing ministries. For our world to embrace a culture of life, we must first heal from the devastation abortion has wreaked.

Give of yourself. There is something empowering and encouraging about giving sacrificially of our time and talents. Sacrificing for the cause of life and the cause of my fellow abortion survivors has made a tremendous difference in my own life. While my efforts may have benefited others, they've also benefited me. Doing my part has given me peace.

I want that same peace for you. Plenty of organizations provide help, healing, and hope, as well as opportunities to further pro-life education, advocacy, and policy change. These are great places that might benefit from your time and talents.

Care Net, Heartbeat International, and the Guiding Star Project, for example, have local centers across the country and even around the world. These organizations benefit greatly from the help of volunteers. (We are always looking for volunteers at The Abortion Survivors Network!) In addition to checking Appendix B, you can also search online for pro-life organizations or pregnancy centers in your area. Sometimes friends and church members can also help you find local opportunities.

Give financially. Providing financial support is a vital way to help make a difference, especially since most pro-life organizations don't have access to any government funding.

Use your voice—and your keyboard. Healing helps you find your voice. So do reading resources like this book and attending pro-life trainings or presentations. Once you're equipped to use your voice, then comes the fun part—using it!

Legislators, whether local or national, need to hear from you. Maybe you have questions about their vote or their stance on an issue. Maybe you simply want to say thank you. Either way, the more you communicate, the more they'll know that an issue is important to you. And after reading this book, you'll likely know more about failed abortions and abortion survivors than most legislators.

There are many ways to communicate with your legislators:

- Send an email. Email is good. Email is read. Sometimes you even get a response!
- Send a letter—or ten.
- Call his or her office every time an abortion-related issue comes up for a vote, or even if it looks like a vote is in the works. Remember to be respectful, even if you vehemently disagree with their stance on abortion.

- When it comes to federal legislators who represent your district or state, begin by contacting their local offices. Develop a relationship with their staff if possible. Once again, expressing thanks or asking questions about their positions is part of this conversation. Find out if they have local town hall meetings you can attend.
- If you're planning a visit to your state (or even the federal) capital, contact your legislator's office well in advance and try to set up a face-to-face meeting. (Many pro-life legislators plan such meetings around March for Life events, which have now expanded beyond Washington, DC, to include many state-level events.) More than ever before, ballot initiatives on abortion are taking shape at the state and local levels. Relationships matter, so work to establish them.

Following the steps and ideas above—starting with difficult conversations and healing—is vital. As you gain confidence, start sending those emails. Write those letters. Call your legislators. Track pro-life legislation or follow organizations that do. Get informed, then get involved! Whether it's on the local, state, or national level, you *can* do this. You *can* make a difference. We can all make a difference *together*!

APPENDIX B

Resources

WHILE A LONE VOICE CAN BE POWERFUL, the thunderous roar of many voices can shake the firmament of our culture. The organizations listed below offer opportunities to add your voice to the roar of those already speaking up for life.

We are blessed to have a diverse group of organizations that serve the pro-life cause. The number is so vast that I could never include them all, so I've tried to highlight organizations from each of the various helping, healing, advocacy, and policy corners of the pro-life movement.

Healing Organizations

THE ABORTION SURVIVORS NETWORK
AbortionSurvivors.org

The Abortion Survivors Network offers healing, support, and community for abortion survivors and their families, and it empowers them to find and use their voices to educate the public about failed abortions and abortion survivors.

REPRODUCTIVE LOSS NETWORK
ReproductiveLossNetwork.org

Reproductive loss includes, but is not limited to, grief after abortion, miscarriage, stillbirth, infertility, and adoption. Reproductive Loss Network offers faith-based training and coaching for those who want to help the grieving, frameworks for healing programs in churches and other organizations, encouragement for helpers through partnerships, and support with abortion pill reversal.

SUPPORT AFTER ABORTION
SupportAfterAbortion.com

In an atmosphere of acceptance and flexibility, Support After Abortion offers an "options-based" approach to healing—an approach that includes both faith-based and secular initiatives for individuals or groups.

SURRENDERING THE SECRET
SurrenderingTheSecret.com

Surrendering the Secret helps women (and men) heal from the hurt of abortion. Abortion affects people from all walks of life, and Surrendering the Secret provides resources for women who've had abortions and opportunities for others to help support these women.

HURT AFTER ABORTION
HurtAfterAbortion.com

Hurt After Abortion provides:

- referrals for legal consultations (if the attorneys decide to take your case, their services are typically free of charge)
- referrals to emotional and spiritual support for women who would like to process their experiences and find healing from the impact of abortion

- assistance in requesting medical records (the right to access your medical records is fundamental to your ability to participate in your own care)

AND THEN THERE WERE NONE
AbortionWorker.com

And Then There Were None is a nonprofit organization started by former Planned Parenthood clinic director Abby Johnson to help abortion clinic workers leave their jobs and find new careers outside the abortion industry.

Help in a Crisis or Unplanned Pregnancy

PROLOVE MINISTRIES
ProLoveMinistries.org

The mission of ProLove Ministries is to help identify blind spots in the pro-life movement and develop comprehensive strategies to promote the value of all life, regardless of race, age, gender, ability, or stage of development.

CARE NET
Care-Net.org

Acknowledging that every human life begins at conception and is worthy of protection, Care Net provides compassion, hope, and help to anyone considering abortion by offering realistic alternatives and Christ-centered support through a life-affirming network of pregnancy centers, churches, organizations, and individuals.

HEARTBEAT INTERNATIONAL
HeartbeatInternational.org

Heartbeat International is a network of pro-life pregnancy resource centers with affiliates in the United States and around the world. Since 1971, Heartbeat has supported, strengthened, and launched pregnancy-help organizations, including pregnancy medical clinics, pregnancy resource centers, maternity homes, and adoption agencies. Heartbeat works with more than 3,000 affiliate locations on six continents to provide alternatives to abortion.

THE GUIDING STAR PROJECT
GuidingStarProject.com

The Guiding Star Project is a nationwide community of care centers that helps women understand, embrace, and love their natural bodies. Guiding Star welcomes all women with a holistic message of appreciation for fertility, childbearing, and family life. It also provides one-stop access to resources that support women's physical, mental, and familial health for a lifetime.

THE GABRIEL PROJECT
GabrielProject.org

The Gabriel Project is a confidential and compassionate outreach to women in distress over an unplanned pregnancy. Relying on local parish communities, the Gabriel Project responds in a loving manner to the needs of the mother-to-be, demonstrating the infinite and healing love of God. A trained Gabriel Angel from a participating church supports a woman's choice for life through friendship, encouragement, and prayer throughout her pregnancy. This Gabriel Angel also helps expectant moms meet practical needs, including clothing, housing, medical care, and counseling.

SAFE HAVEN BABY BOXES
SHBB.org

The mission of Safe Haven Baby Boxes is to prevent illegal abandonment of newborns by raising awareness, offering a 24-hour hotline for mothers in crisis, and providing a last-resort option for women.

Adoption Support for Birth Mothers

ABIDING LOVE ADOPTIONS
AbidingLoveAdopt.com

Abiding Love Adoptions is an agency that specializes in infant adoption. They are located and licensed in Georgia, Florida, and South Carolina, and they have a mission to love and support birth mothers throughout the open adoption process. Abiding Love offers continued support to the birth mother after the placement of her child for adoption.

Sidewalk Counseling and Prayer

Sidewalk advocacy is peaceful, prayerful presence on the public sidewalks outside an abortion clinic. Information for women is provided through signs, written materials, and loving communication (no yelling or condemning). Sidewalk counselors offer information about community resources, free ultrasounds, and pregnancy tests. Many describe such advocacy as "ground zero"— a last chance to reach an abortion-minded woman with information that can not only save her child's life but also protect her from abortion's physical, emotional, and spiritual impact.

SIDEWALK ADVOCATES FOR LIFE
SidewalkAdvocates.org

Sidewalk Advocates for Life trains, equips, and supports individuals and groups across the United States and around the world in sidewalk advocacy at abortion facilities, offering loving, life-affirming alternatives to all.

40 DAYS FOR LIFE
40DaysForLife.com

An internationally coordinated forty-day campaign, 40 Days for Life aims to end abortion locally through prayer, fasting, community outreach, and peaceful all-day vigils in front of abortion facilities.

Faith and Family Resources

PRIESTS FOR LIFE
PriestsForLife.org

Priests for Life galvanizes the clergy to preach, teach, and mobilize their people more effectively in the effort to end abortion and euthanasia. Priests for Life represents a family of ministries that reach and enrich every aspect of the pro-life movement, for clergy and laity alike, in a wide variety of activities. Priests are not ordained for themselves, but for the people. Therefore, in activating clergy, Priests for Life activates all segments of the church, the pro-life movement, and society at large in the defense of life.

FAMILY RESEARCH COUNCIL
FRC.org

Family Research Council's mission is to advance faith, family, and freedom in public policy and in culture from a biblical worldview.

FOCUS ON THE FAMILY
FocusOnTheFamily.com

Through radio broadcasts, websites, simulcasts, conferences, interactive forums, magazines, books, counseling, and much more, Focus on the Family equips parents, children, and spouses to thrive in an ever-changing, ever more complicated world.

Secular Pro-Life Organizations

SECULAR PRO-LIFE
SecularProLife.org

Secular Pro-Life has a three-part mission: to advance secular arguments against abortion; to create space for atheists, agnostics, and other secularists interested in anti-abortion work; and to build inter-faith coalitions of people interested in advancing secular arguments.

Educational/Advocacy Organizations

AMERICAN ASSOCIATION OF PRO-LIFE OBSTETRICIANS AND GYNECOLOGISTS
AAPLOG.org

The American Association of Pro-Life Obstetricians and Gynecologists (AAPLOG) exists to encourage and equip its members and other concerned medical practitioners to provide an evidence-based rationale for defending the lives of both the pregnant mother and her preborn child. AAPLOG is the largest organization of pro-life obstetricians and gynecologists in the world. Their goal is that all women, regardless of race, creed, or national origin, will be empowered to make healthy and life-affirming choices.

CHARLOTTE LOZIER INSTITUTE
LozierInstitute.org

The Charlotte Lozier Institute is committed to bringing the power of science, medicine, and research to bear in life-related policymaking, media, and debates to promote a culture and polity of life. (The organization offers a very helpful fact sheet called "Questions and Answers on Born-Alive Abortion Survivors," which is available at lozierinstitute.org/questions-and-answers-on -born-alive-abortion-survivors.)

MEN FOR LIFE
MenForLife.org

Men for Life's mission is to protect and expand human rights by encouraging men to be informed, active, and purposeful defenders of life.

Policy Organizations Related to Abortion Survivors

SUSAN B. ANTHONY PRO-LIFE AMERICA
SBAProLife.org

Susan B. Anthony Pro-Life America (formerly known as the Susan B. Anthony List) is a nationwide network of more than one million Americans who combine politics with policy, investing heavily in voter education to ensure that pro-life Americans know where their lawmakers stand on protecting the unborn. They are also involved in issue advocacy, advancing pro-life laws through direct lobbying and grassroots campaigns.

THE ABORTION SURVIVORS EDUCATION AND POLICY CENTER
EducationAndPolicyCenter.com

The Abortion Survivors Education and Policy Center advocates for policies that protect the unborn and abortion survivors, humanizing the victims of abortion in a way that no one else can.

Books about Abortion Survivors

- *An Accidental Life* by Pamela Binnings Ewen (fiction)
- *Gianna: Aborted, and Lived to Tell about It* by Jessica Shaver Renshaw
- *In That Secret Place: An Abortion Survivor's Story* by Terri Kellogg and Hope Hoffman
- *Lodene: A True Story* by June Botha
- *Miracles Happen in the Wilderness: A Book of Rememberance* by Robin Dawn Sertell
- *"My Ma Ma": The Inspiring Story of an Orphan Girl Given a Chance to Have a Life* by Betty Genter
- *October Baby: A Novel* by Eric Wilson and Theresa Preston (adapted into the 2011 film *October Baby*)
- *Survivor: An Abortion Survivor's Surprising Story of Choosing Forgiveness and Finding Redemption* by Claire Culwell with Lois and Steve Rabey
- *You Carried Me: A Daughter's Memoir* by Melissa Ohden

ACKNOWLEDGMENTS

GOD HAS BROUGHT TOGETHER AN AMAZING TEAM of people that made this groundbreaking book possible. *Lord, I thank You.*

My sincerest thanks to Wes Yoder and the team at Ambassador Speakers Bureau and Literary Agency for believing in my voice and helping amplify abortion survivors' voices while at the same time saving lives and bringing healing to the hurting.

To the editorial and marketing teams at Focus on the Family: It has been an honor to get to know you over the years and work alongside you, sowing hope and truth that change lives and our culture.

To my friend and fellow pro-life advocate Abby Johnson: I'm grateful and humbled by your gracious foreword and your continued support of my work.

Words can't begin to express how much I appreciate all the contributors who told us their stories. Entrusting Cindy Lambert and me with such vulnerable stories is an honor for us both.

Speaking of Cindy, it has been quite a journey for us in creating this book! Little could we have imagined at the beginning of the pandemic how life and this book would be such an exercise in dogged perseverance. You have given survivors a voice, Cindy, and done so with such respect and care. I'm grateful to have collaborated on this with you.

While this book gives abortion survivors and women who experienced failed abortions a voice, I want to acknowledge in particular some of those who will read it:

To women like my birth mother, Ruth, who have experienced failed abortions: You are not alone. You deserve to experience healing, support, and love.

To those who have carried the secrets and shame of failed abortions in your families for generations: I know it's difficult to break the cycle of secrets and abortion, but your courage can change generations!

To second- and third-generation abortion survivors who are alive today because of a survivor in their family: You are also not alone! You are joined by others who are alive today because an abortion failed to end the life of a parent, grandparent, or great-grandparent.

To adoptive families like my own who have opened their hearts and homes to abortion survivors, not knowing what their future may hold but knowing who holds their future: Thank you.

Last but not least, I want to acknowledge and challenge our culture—a culture that has been so impacted by abortion that it attempts to shame abortion survivors into silent submission. Whether or not you've been personally impacted by abortion, I challenge you to read this book. Abortion survivors deserve to be healed, empowered, and equipped. They deserve to be seen and heard.

NOTES

CHAPTER 1 | WHISPERED SECRETS

1. Melissa Ohden, *You Carried Me: A Daughter's Memoir* (Walden, NY: Plough Publishing House, 2017), 22–23.
2. Liz Jeffries and Rick Edmonds, "Abortion: The Dreaded Complication," *Philadelphia Inquirer*, August 2, 1981, https://web.archive.org/web/20210712064915/https:/digitalcollections.library.cmu.edu/awweb/awarchive?type=file&item=693589.
3. Jeffries, "Abortion."
4. Jeffries, "Abortion."
5. Annalisa Merelli, "There Is No Such Thing as an 'Abortion Survivor,'" *Quartz*, February 25, 2019, https://qz.com/1556779/who-are-abortion-survivors.
6. Anna Reynolds, "Abortion Survivor Accounts 'Fairy Tales,' Claims Pro-Abortion Irish Politician," *Live Action News*, December 17, 2018, https://www.liveaction.org/news/abortion-survivor-fairy-tales-irish.
7. Calla Hales, "'Born Alive' Abortion Bills Are Based on Nothing but Propaganda,'" *Rewire News Group*, April 12, 2019, https://rewirenewsgroup.com/article/2019/04/12/born-alive-abortion-bills-are-based-on-nothing-but-propaganda.

CHAPTER 2 | MORE THAN A CHOICE: MY STORY

1. Liz Jeffries and Rick Edmonds, "Abortion: The Dreaded Complication," *Philadelphia Inquirer*, August 2, 1981, https://web.archive.org/web/20210712064915/https:/digitalcollections.library.cmu.edu/awweb/awarchive?type=file&item=693589.
2. Jeffries, "Abortion."
3. Jeffries, "Abortion."

4. Erin Fuchs, "Abortion Doctor Accused of 'Snipping' the Necks of Hundreds of Live Babies," Yahoo! Finance, April 9, 2013, https://finance .yahoo.com/news/abortion-doctor-accused-snipping-necks-223751236 .html.

5. Wesley J. Smith, "Why Born-Alive Abortion Survivor Protection Laws Are Needed," *National Review*, February 25, 2021, https://www.nationalreview .com/corner/why-born-alive-abortion-survivor-protection-laws-are-needed.

6. Anne Lim, "Call to Arms over 27 Babies Left to Die," *Eternity News*, November 30, 2017, https://www.eternitynews.com.au/australia/call-to -arms-over-27-babies-left-to-die.

CHAPTER 3 | A LIFE REDEFINED: PRISCILLA'S STORY

1. Priscilla shared her testimony with the help of Dave Franco on the website of the organization And Then There Were None at https://abortionworker .com/abortion-industry-quitter-of-the-month-priscilla-hurley. Parts of this chapter and Priscilla's testimony on that website use many of the same phrases since both were developed from Priscilla's own words and interviews with her. Used by permission.

CHAPTER 4 | THE BROKEN CHAIN: MICHELLE'S STORY

1. Paul Stark, "The Coat Hanger Is a Lie: Why the 'Back-Alley Abortion' Argument Fails," Minnesota Citizens Concerned for Life, October 19, 2017, https://www.mccl.org/post/2017/10/19/the-coat-hanger-is-a-lie -why-the-back-alley-abortion-argument-for-legalized-abortion-does.

CHAPTER 7 | THE MYSTERIOUS BOND: JENNIFER'S STORY

1. "Placenta Previa," Mayo Clinic, https://www.mayoclinic.org/diseases -conditions/placenta-previa/symptoms-causes/syc-20352768.

2. "Jennifer Callender, Twin Abortion Survivor," Faces of Choice, July 21, 2020, YouTube, 5:11, https://youtu.be/-pvHW_EB4Ic.

CHAPTER 8 | COLD WATER TO A THIRSTY SOUL: JULIAN'S STORY

1. "Ayurvedic Medicine: In Depth," National Center for Complementary and Integrative Health, updated January 2019, https://www.nccih.nih.gov/health /ayurvedic-medicine-in-depth.

CHAPTER 10 | THE STRENGTH OF HOPE: HOPE'S STORY

1. Terri Kellogg and Hope Hoffman, *In That Secret Place: An Abortion Survivor's Story* (Maitland, FL: Xulon, 2012), 30.

2. Kellogg, *In That Secret Place*, 31.

3. Kellogg, *In That Secret Place*, 29.

CHAPTER 13 | THE SECOND CHANCE: ZECHARIAH'S STORY

1. Heartbeat International's Abortion Pill Rescue Network reports that over three thousand babies—and counting—have been saved through the use of abortion pill reversal (https://www.heartbeatinternational.org/images /HeartbeatServices/ImpactReports/2021_APRN_CIR.pdf).

CHAPTER 15 | NO MORE SECRETS

1. Dr. Stephen Hammond is board certified as an ob-gyn through the American Board of Obstetrics and Gynecology, he has been a fellow at the American College of Obstetricians and Gynecologists, and he serves as the medical director of clinical research at The Jackson Clinic in Jackson, Tennessee.
2. Frederica Mathewes-Green, "Seeking Abortion's Middle Ground," *Washington Post*, July 28, 1996, https://www.washingtonpost.com/archive /opinions/1996/07/28/seeking-abortions-middle-ground/f04dd815-967d -4dbe-a28f-6e1b73ea6d1f.
3. Malala Yousafzai, "16th Birthday Speech at the United Nations," July 12, 2013, https://malala.org/newsroom/malala-un-speech.

Stand with others for life.

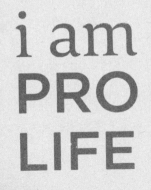

Join our online community.

Facebook.com/FocusOnLife

Instagram.com/i.am.prolife

FOCUS ON THE FAMILY

CP1912

PROGRAM

Life can *be* when moms can *see*.

When you say *yes* to becoming an
Option Ultrasound Life Advocate, you
empower pregnant mothers to *see*
life. Your ongoing support provides
ultrasounds to moms considering
abortion. You help them see their babies,
hear their heartbeats, and choose life.

**Your monthly
giving matters.**

FOCUS ON THE FAMILY.

CP1913